For Strasbourg

For Strasbourg

Conversations of Friendship and Philosophy

JACQUES DERRIDA

Edited and Translated by Pascale-Anne Brault and Michael Naas

FORDHAM UNIVERSITY PRESS

New York 2014

This book brings together four texts that were originally published in French under the following titles: "Le lieu dit: Strasbourg," by Jacques Derrida, in *Penser à Strasbourg* © Éditions Galilée, 2004; "Dialogue entre Jacques Derrida, Philippe Lacoue-Labarthe, and Jean-Luc Nancy," in *Rue Descartes*, no. 52 (2006): 86–99, © Succession Derrida/Succession Lacoue-Labarthe/Jean-Luc Nancy; "Ouverture," discussion avec Jean-Luc Nancy, *Rue Descartes* 45 (2004): 26–55, © Succession Derrida/Jean-Luc Nancy; "Résponsabilité du sens a venir," conversation avec Jean-Luc Nancy, in *Sens en tous sens: Autour des travaux de Jean-Luc Nancy*, © Éditions Galilée, 2004.

Fordham University Press also publishes its books in a variety of electronic formats. Some content that appears in print may not be available in electronic books.

Library of Congress Cataloging-in-Publication Data is available from the publisher.

Published in the United States of America
16 15 14   5 4 3 2 1
First edition

Contents

Translators' Preface   vii

1. The Place Name(s)—Strasbourg (2004)   I
2. Discussion Between Jacques Derrida, Philippe Lacoue-Labarthe,
    and Jean-Luc Nancy (2004)   17
3. Opening (2003)   31
4. Responsibility—Of the Sense to Come (2002)   56

Notes   87

Translator's Preface

Jacques Derrida loved the city of Strasbourg. Though he never lived or held a teaching position there, from the early 1970s right up to his death in 2004 Derrida traveled frequently to this city on the Franco-German border just over three hundred miles from Paris for everything from lectures, conferences, and colloquia to dissertation defenses, book signings, and artistic events. Attracted from the very beginning to this city because of its unique location and history, its multiplicity of languages and cultures, over time Derrida came to find Strasbourg an even more special place as organizations and movements that were dear to him came to be housed in or identified with the city, from the European Parliament to the International Parliament of Writers and the Parliament of Philosophers.

But it was above all friends who drew Derrida back to Strasbourg for more than three decades: friends in the municipality, friends in the artistic community, but especially friends in the university—beginning with Jean-Luc Nancy and Philippe Lacoue-Labarthe. It was through these friends that Strasbourg, City of Parliaments and City of Refuge par excellence, became for Derrida a city of conversation and hospitality, indeed, of friendship and philosophy.

It was thus absolutely fitting that in June 2004, just four months before his death, the Parliament of Philosophers and the Department of Philosophy at Marc Bloch University, where Nancy and Lacoue-Labarthe were both teaching, would invite Jacques Derrida to Strasbourg for three days of meetings and conversations around his work. From June

7 to 9, 2004, Derrida thus participated in a series of events, from a discussion with high school teachers from the Lycée Fustel de Coulanges about the teaching of philosophy to a tribute paid to him at Marc Bloch University and a public discussion with Isabelle Baladine-Howald on the topic of friendship at the Kléber Bookstore. On the evening of June 8, 2004, Derrida also gave what was to be his last lecture in France, "Of the 'Sovereign Good'—Europe in Want of Sovereignty."[1] The collection *For Strasbourg: Conversations of Friendship and Philosophy* grew out of these events in Strasbourg, though Derrida himself never planned such a publication.

The work begins with the long tribute Derrida paid the city of Strasbourg during his three days there in June 2004. Titled "The Place Name(s)—Strasbourg" (though it could easily bear the title or the dedication "For Strasbourg"), the essay recounts in great detail, and in very moving terms, Derrida's affection for the city of Strasbourg, his many visits to this city, and, especially, his decades-long intellectual friendship with Nancy, Lacoue-Labarthe, and others. Through reflections, anecdotes, and shared memories with these two philosopher friends, Derrida is able to paint a fascinating portrait of French intellectual life over a thirty-year period, with stories about the many conferences he attended in Strasbourg, his testy relationship with the French university system, his break with Tel Quel, his association with Éditions Galilée, the founding of GREPH and of the International College of Philosophy, the importance of conferences at Cerisy-la-Salle, and so on.

This essay is a great testament to the importance of Strasbourg as a city of hospitality and of refuge for contemporary thought and, especially, for the kind of philosophy that was being done by Derrida, Nancy, and Lacoue-Labarthe and that could find a home nowhere else. Originally published in the appropriately titled volume *Penser à Strasbourg* (*Thinking of/in Strasbourg*, 2004), the essay bears witness not just to Derrida's deep attachment to this border city but to his continuing interrogation of the relationship between thought and place, philosophy and language, language and nationality, philosophy and friendship.[2] It thus raises a series of important philosophical, political, and ethical questions that might all be placed under the aegis of what Derrida came to call in his seminars of the 1980s "philosophical nationalities and nationalism."

But "The Place Name(s)—Strasbourg" is first of all a work of memory and of friendship. Punctuated by names and memories, it reads like a long good-bye to a city and its inhabitants, the last episode in Derrida's three-decade adventure in "shuttle philosophy" between Paris and Strasbourg. Written at an almost breathless pace, with long sentences often interrupted by asides and parenthetical remarks, the essay betrays Derrida's anxiety to say it all, to express fully his gratitude, to include every name and recount every experience having to do with Strasbourg. The essay bespeaks Derrida's unique relationship to the city of Strasbourg and to the two friends or fellow "musketeers" who became major figures in their own right in contemporary philosophy and literary theory.[3]

The second text included in this collection has its origin in the same three days of homage and celebration in Strasbourg, and it brings Derrida together once again with Jean-Luc Nancy and Philippe Lacoue-Labarthe. During the final day of Derrida's visit, a session was organized at Marc Bloch University around the work of four doctoral students, who presented their work and discussed it with Derrida.[4] This session was then followed by a roundtable discussion between Derrida, Nancy, and Lacoue-Labarthe that took as its point of departure these student presentations but that then went on to address questions related to the three thinkers' own work, questions, for example, regarding Heidegger and his politics, community and generation, and, most poignantly, death, finitude, mourning, survival, and immortality. We thus hear Derrida, four months before his death, conversing with Strasbourg's two most famous philosophers about the all too relevant and pressing questions of legacy, the archive, the afterlife, and immortality.

First published in the journal *Rue Descartes*, this wide-ranging discussion between these three philosopher friends combines sharp insights into one another's work with personal anecdotes, friendly ribbing, and good humor. It is the kind of serious but also playful discussion that is possible only among close friends.[5] As the editors of *Rue Descartes* say in their introduction to this exchange: "No 'subject' had been determined for this conversation beforehand. The three 'philosopher-friends' thus came together. It would be for the last time."

This might well have been a fitting way to conclude *For Strasbourg*, with the final conversation between Derrida, Nancy, and Lacoue-Labarthe on topics ranging from community to the afterlife. But because the philosophical conversations between Derrida and his two most famous Strasbourgian interlocutors will continue on in their writings long after their deaths, we have the opportunity, even the obligation, to go back to other conversations from earlier times, times when the end was not already casting its shadow over everything. It is for this reason that two additional public conversations between Derrida and Nancy have been included in this volume. The first of these, entitled simply "Opening," is a transcription of the opening session, on November 4, 2003, of three days of celebration marking the twenty-year anniversary of the International College of Philosophy, of which Derrida was one of the founders.[6] We hear Derrida discussing with Jean-Luc Nancy and others, including Hélène Cixous and Michel Deguy, the political and cultural circumstances surrounding the founding of the International College of Philosophy, the place of philosophy in the French university and in other academic institutions, the sometimes conflicted relationship between the members of the College and the university, and the importance of the College as a place of refuge for university professors and, especially, high school teachers of philosophy. The conversation sheds a great deal of light both on this counter-institution called the International College of Philosophy, which, now more than thirty years later, is still thriving, and on the importance of philosophy more generally in France from the late 1960s into the new millennium. (It is worth noting that both this chapter and the previous one were first published in *Rue Descartes*, the journal of the International College of Philosophy.)

The fourth and final chapter of *For Strasbourg* is a conversation between Derrida and Nancy that took place at a conference devoted to Nancy's work—once again at the International College of Philosophy—on January 18 and 19, 2002.[7] The conversation begins with the question of the relationship between responsibility and the event, the question of whether one can ever bear or assume responsibility for an event, that is, for something that happens in some sense without or before any subject, without or before anyone's decision. This question provides the terms for then rethinking a whole host of other questions, from that of the gift and of debt to questions of the relationship between philosophy and Christianity, the meaning of revelation, sense, and guilt, the commonly assumed philosophical distinction between the human and the animal, and so on. If Derrida and Nancy ultimately agree on many issues in the course of this long exchange, they often disagree very strongly on one another's approach. We hear Nancy, for example, expressing skepticism about Derrida's emphasis in recent works on the human/animal distinction, and we hear Derrida professing his profound resistance or allergy to terms such as *sense, world, creation, freedom,* and *community,* which are at the center of Nancy's thought. But, once again, what comes across here despite these differences, perhaps even because of them, is the deep friendship—the philosophical friendship—between these two thinkers.

All four of the texts collected in *For Strasbourg* are thus relatively "late texts" in the corpus of Jacques Derrida, with three of the four taking place during the final year of his life. This lends the volume a somewhat melancholic tone at times, especially in the two works that originated in Strasbourg just months before Derrida's death. (Derrida knew that he was gravely ill, and his friends did as well, when he visited Strasbourg in June 2004.) But what comes across most clearly, in the end, is not his impending death and not some wistful nostalgia for a bygone age but the intellectual vigor and vibrancy of friends who have shared a great deal and who have chosen to continue to discuss topics of philosophical interest to the three of them right up until the end. These texts should thus be read not just for what they reveal about Derrida's thinking near the end of his life but for what they teach us about his thought in general. Indeed, these texts present in very clear and often personal terms many important aspects of Derrida's thought, from his early thinking of the trace and of speech acts to his work in the 1980s and 1990s on friendship, the gift, and religion, to his later thought on the archive and on legacy.

For Strasbourg is a testament to the important place of Strasbourg for contemporary thought and to Derrida's great affection for this city and for the two thinkers most closely identified with it. It is also a testament to an extraordinary period of philosophical activity in France more generally and to the philosophical friendships that made so much of what happened possible.

For Strasbourg

CHAPTER ONE

The Place Name(s)—Strasbourg
(2004)

"Der Ort sagt . . ."

This is going to be about thinking [*il y va de la pensée*], to be sure, about thinking as a going concern, about whether it's going well or poorly (just try to translate this into another language, into German, for example: *la pensée comme elle va*).[1] It is going to be about the thinking writing [*l'écriture pensante*] that traverses philosophy, literature, poetry, music, theater, the visual arts—as well as politics—and the rest.

Why begin with such a dry, cold, abstract statement? If I insist on saying that, first of all and finally, everything will have had to do, in the last analysis, for me, for us, for you, with thinking and with writing, whatever this may mean and whatever it may entail, it is in part in order to protect myself. To protect myself against myself. It is in order to try to stem the flow, in truth, to stem the tears of emotion, of gratitude, of love and of friendship, of nostalgia as well, indeed of melancholy, which would otherwise overwhelm my words here today in Strasbourg. My tone should not be one of an eschatological pathos in philosophy. This is not a last meeting with my friends from Strasbourg. That is at least my hope, and I mean it with all my heart.

If I thus begin by recalling thinking or writing, it is not because I still know, after all these years, what these words mean or, at least for us, what they will have one day had to mean. No, it is so that through the effusion we do not lose sight, in the so very rich landscape of our common memory, of this certainty and this truth: what called me from the beginning to Strasbourg, what attracted me to your city (which I have never been able to consider, and for decades now, apart from the concrete existence, from the bodies and shapes, from the faces, of my first and dearest friends in thinking and writing, Philippe Lacoue-Labarthe and Claire, Jean-Luc and Hélène Nancy, Lucien Braun, Isabelle Baladine Howald, and others still, Paola Marrati, Francis Guibal, Daniel Payot, Denis Guénoun, who, in November 1992 and under the aegis of the Department of Philosophy, organized with Jean-Luc Nancy, Philippe Lacoue-Labarthe, and Daniel Payot, at the meeting of the Carrefour des littératures européennes in Strasbourg, presided over by Christian Salmon, very rich discussions published under the title *Penser l'Europe à ses frontières* [*Thinking Europe at Its Borders*]²), what has brought us together here, what has made of my love for this city one of the blessings of my life, was first and always, among us, among all those whom I have just named, the uncompromising injunction of thinking. Nothing would have taken place, in this place Strasbourg, without this, without this injunction, which was also a desire to think and to write, each in his or her own way, philosophy, on philosophy, but also on literature, poetry, theater, music, and the visual arts, and then through all of that, since what I am speaking of is the love of a city, of a metropolis that is not just any metropolis in France and in Europe, since it is municipalities that I also wish to thank, through all of that, as I said, there was politics, the political, which we will have occasion to discuss again. For what Strasbourg, the city and my friends, my first hosts and my hosts of today have once again given me the chance to share with them, as I have never done with others, is also, and I will recall a few moments of this, a political experience. An experience that has been not only academic and cultural but political: national, European, and international.

All of this—thinking, speaking, writing *in* Strasbourg, *to* Strasbourg— would not have been possible, let me repeat, and would not have been political, without that initial impetus, which Philippe Lacoue-Labarthe, Jean-Luc Nancy, and myself understood from the very beginning was calling us together, calling us to live and to come together, to *convene* and *concur* in something like a synagogue. As you know, that is the first meaning of the word: a synagogue (*synagōgē*) is the gathering, the place (name) or locality [*le lieu dit*] that says [*dit*] or dictates coming together, the place where one comes and goes to meet up with others, the space where our steps lead us and where we walk side by side. In the Jewish Algerian milieu of my childhood, one used to say, curiously, "temple" in place of "synagogue." As if to hide this word by veiling it, by reforming it.

Strasbourg is also for me the blindfolded synagogue of your cathedral. I idolize this idol, this woman bereft of sight and voice, this mute and sorrowful figure. It was she whom I visited the very first time, only to notice that the name on the postcard reproductions of this image (those printed by the cathedral) is not "The Blindfolded Synagogue" but simply, as if this were obvious, "Synagogue, Allegory of the Old Testament (first quarter of the thirteenth century)." Hélène Nancy, whom I wish to thank here, just sent me another postcard that reads "The Synagogue, 'Old Testament Law.'" For beyond the insult or calumny that is no doubt insinuated, namely, that of a certain Jewish blindness to the truth of Christian revelation, it seemed to me that this blindfolded synagogue was calling out to us, addressing to us a silent request, the three of us and all those close to us. As only a woman can do, she would not be naively asking us: what is the truth of revelation, what is sight, what is the veil or unveiling? What is Judaism, Christianity, or Islam in the Europe of today and of tomorrow? She presses us with a preliminary question: what does it mean to bind or to band, to get it up—over the eyes [*bander*], to blindfold the eyes or have eyes blindfolded for thinking, writing, philosophy, politics, existence in general?

This question also comes to us through the trial of a certain Judeity that will have always been a deep and constant concern for the three of us, each in his own way, Jean-Luc the Jew, Philippe the Judeo-Catholic, and I who am, as everyone knows, half-Catholic, half-Calvinist. The "Jewish question," in all its dimensions—religious, philosophical, political—resonates in Strasbourg in a very singular way. Not only because of the proximity to Germany and the memory of Nazism, but also because of the active presence of a remarkable and vibrant Jewish community with very old roots. Hélène Nancy often brought me to *La Petite-France* and to places where this Jewish community is concentrated. Our friend Hélène Cixous, who is at once Ashkenazi and Sephardic, was invited a few weeks ago (as I myself once was) to the Kléber Bookstore by Isabelle Baladine Howald. Accompanied by Eve, her mother, and Anne, her daughter, she was looking for the traces of her Strasbourgeois ancestors. And it is again she who suggested to me yesterday that *synagogue* was *la Chose même*, the Cause, *das Ding*, the Thing [in English in the original], that is, as Heidegger recalls and never ceased to ponder, the place where one gathers to speak, to debate, to *parlement* around some litigation. And then I think of the singular relation between the Church and the State in Alsace. And it seems to me not insignificant that one of my hosts and friends today at the University of Strasbourg is Gérard Bensussan, who, I will never forget, generously invited me to Aix-en Provence to discuss nothing other than the relationship between Scholem and Rosenzweig with regard to the Hebrew language, and who participated with Jean-Luc and others in a conference on Judeity in Paris, and who has become in everyone's eyes a leading expert in Judeo-German philosophy, and not just in the work of the great Rosenzweig.

Since I am playing a bit at circling around your famous cathedral and this blindfolded synagogue, I ask you to allow someone who has written a great deal on eyes, on blind men and on blinding in the history of the arts, on the singularity of women and of women mourners in this story, to go on just a little longer. I recall in passing that *synagōgē* was first the Greek translation of the Hebrew *knesset*, which means precisely the place or house of gathering (*bet-ha-knesset*), in short, the Parliament. After the Temple was destroyed and during the captivity in Babylon, synagogues sprang up everywhere during the diaspora. The Parliament, the synagogue, the *knesset*, is, in the end, not only *la même chose*, that is, the same thing, but *la Cause, la Chose même, das Ding,* the Thing. And so Strasbourg, the city of Parliaments (European Parliament, International Parliament of Writers, Parliament of Philosophers), Strasbourg as the city of Parliament in general, of the Parliament par excellence, of the Parliament itself, becomes at once a synagogue, a *knesset*, and the Thing itself. If someone today were to retranslate "the blindfolded synagogue" by "the blindfolded *Knesset*," and if, in order to give the Knesset of Jerusalem its sight back, this person were to appeal not to the United States but to Europe, whose Strasbourg, seat of the Council of Europe and then of the European Assembly, is to my eyes the metonymy, and thus the other Knesset, I bet that, unfortunately, this imprudent person would be deemed an anti-Semite, if not a neo-Judeophobe. For one of the most revolting and intolerable things about our time is that one can no longer criticize Sharon and the Israeli politics coming out of the Knesset and supported by the United States without being accused of anti-Semitic racism or, as one says today, of Judeophobia. And even of complicity with the terrifying resurgence of anti-Semitism in Europe. It is as if the forgetting of the Shoah were on the side of those who criticize this Israeli politics supported by the United States, rather than, as I myself believe, on the side of those who conduct and support this disastrous politics, which is unfortunately not completely unrelated to this reawakening of the anti-Semitic monster, even if this does not explain everything, far from it, and does not justify in the least either of the two anti-Semitic racisms, Judeophobia or Islamophobia. But I am getting away from my topic, as always.

What my first friends and first hosts of Strasbourg, Philippe Lacoue-Labarthe, Jean-Luc Nancy, and those close to them, taught me to think, as early as their first invitation some thirty-five years ago (in short, almost our entire adult lives), is that thinking, what I call here by this at once modest, abstract, and pompous word *thinking*, the thinking that traverses and exceeds philosophy, literature, poetry, music, theater, drawing, and painting—as well as politics—this thinking would not think, it would not give anything to be thought, it would not let itself be thought, without the body of love, of friendship, of hospitality, without the experience of the gift at the limits of the possible and the impossible. I would venture to claim that the one thing of which we are certain, the three of us and those who have accompanied us during these Strasbourgian decades (but I will get to this, Strasbourg was also a radiating center that sent us, I insist on saying *sent* us, all over the world, to Paris first of all but then throughout Europe and onto every continent), is that without the concern for thinking while writing that has traversed the three of us with the *same* stroke, the same trait [*trait*]—even if the same, as we know, is not the identical—without the attraction of this trait that attracted the three of us to one another and all of us to Strasbourg, our friendship would have made—how shall I put it?—no sense at all (in all the senses of this word *sense*, as Jean-Luc Nancy would say); it would not have stood a chance. In any case, inversely, I know that without this friendship I myself would have never dared move forward in what I still call, to say it quickly, thinking and writing. But because I knew I would not have the time, because this is neither the place nor the moment, because this infinitely overdetermined genealogy would call for an interminable analysis, I decided to restrict myself, in a rather crude and hardly philosophical way, to anecdotes and thus not to take up, either from up close or from afar, the many writings whose content nonetheless forms the very mainspring of the rich experience I have been speaking about.

I have just, in a no doubt rather abusive and unfaithful way, privileged, as I also thought I had to, our trio. But before giving in to the desire—I am not saying to the duty—of memory, before recounting a few stories, I do not want to betray or pass over in silence all those who remain inseparable from our common adventure and from the long journey that leads always from Strasbourg to Strasbourg. I will acknowledge them along the way and express to them all my gratitude.

Rest assured, I will not subject you to the long version of what were my loves, my love for your city, which for no one in the world is simply one great metropolis among others since it is at once the capital of Europe, in a certain sense, and a border city, a city that was constantly expropriated and reappropriated, an open city, open to more than one language, a city of refuge even before the International Parliament of Writers, which was founded right here (I will say a word about this in a moment), reinvented the biblical and medieval institution of cities of refuge; a city of political speech as well, of the freedom of public speech, a city, in a word, dare I say, of *parliamentary* speech, of a speech that democratically argues, dialogues, discusses, deliberates, and "parliaments" with the other. And to "parliament" is not only to speak or to take up speech; it is to leave speech to the other and to listen. City of parliamentary speech, city of "parliament" [*parlement*] therefore.

Parlement is an ambiguous word. It is freighted with a political or unconscious charge that is formidable, not only because of what the crisis of parliamentary representation will have engendered in this century from at least the 1920s onward and not only because the signifier lets itself be invaded or perverted in so many ways: *parle m'en donc, de Strasbourg*, "speak to me, then, of Strasbourg," *le parle-ment, la parole ment*, "speaking lies, speech lies," the *parlementer*, the speaking, becoming often a *parlementir*, a speaking of lies. But *parlement*, despite or because of all this, remains a magnificent word. We should substitute it for *parole*, so long as we understand *parlement* as a *parler*, a speaking, an act of speaking, a *speech act* [in English in the original], a speech in act, even the act of giving speech or giving one's word: as for what I am doing right now, let's imagine that I were to call this not a discourse or a speech but a *parlement*, a *parlement* that, like any *parlement*, tries to welcome more than one voice in its speech, in a given or sworn word that also engages one, let me repeat it, to leave speech to the other, to listen as much as to talk. The *parlement* that I am delivering here recalls that in my generation, in the course of these last decades, Strasbourg, this parliamentary city par excellence, will have hosted the European Parliament, the International Parliament of Writers, and now the new Parliament of Philosophers, which you had the wonderful initiative to inaugurate this year. I had the incredible honor and opportunity to speak and to *parlement* at each of these, without forgetting, of course, the Parliamentary Assembly of the Council of Europe, where I was also given the chance to speak.

When I think of what counts most in my life, Strasbourg will have been a city of refuge for the Algerian exile who I am and who never felt quite at home in Paris, especially in relation to the institutions of the university, of philosophy, culture, and the media in general. Since I've just named my country of origin, allow me to evoke in just a couple of words the singular experience, yet again parliamentary, that I had one day here in Strasbourg somewhere around 1995 or 1996. During a round-table discussion at the International Parliament of Writers on Algeria and the terrorism that was rife there at the time, I found myself on stage next to a young Algerian academic who had lived her entire life in the house and even the bedroom of my childhood in El-Biar. When my parents left their house in 1962 they entrusted it to this young Algerian woman's parents, who were neighbors of ours. In the course of a very moving testimony, she recounted how a new wave of Algerian terrorism had just forced her to seek refuge in France, where a university in Paris and, on that particular day, Strasbourg had welcomed her.

Rest assured, as I said, I am not going to tell you everything about what will have been, for more than thirty-five years, my Strasbourgian nostalgia. I say nostalgia because if I have lived here what are among the happiest and most intense moments of my life as a traveler and wandering philosopher, I've never lived in Strasbourg and, in a certain sense, I have always dreamed of doing so.

Philippe and Jean-Luc claim that I was in Strasbourg before ever coming here. They even recount what they hold to be our first encounters, in person or through texts, around 1970. But the ambiguous privilege of age allows me to go much further back into the past. More than ten years earlier, in 1959, having just taken up my first teaching assignment as instructor for the final year of high school and hypokhâgne in Le Mans, my friend from the École Normale Supérieure and then my colleague at Le Mans, our common friend Gérard Genette, said to me upon my arrival: "It's too bad, you just missed one of our most brilliant students, a young man named Philippe Lacoue-Labarthe, who has just left us for Bordeaux, where he is following his father, the principal of a high school." I got to meet his father much later, right here, when Philippe was defending his dissertation. From my vantage point in the jury, I could see what Philippe, who was facing us, could not: the tears of his father at the moment his great thinker of a son recalled the memory of his mother.

Since Le Mans, the name of Lacoue-Labarthe has been engraved in my memory. I recall being so delighted the day when, even before meeting him, I admired one of his first publications. What filled me with joy was at once recognizing the qualities Genette had told me about and sensing between us, already, a proximity that was for me so rare and so reassuring.

Philippe and Jean-Luc recall our first encounters, beginning in 1970, and I will let them recount the highlights. Even before the conference they had organized on rhetoric, I had already corresponded with Jean-Luc, whose first texts, which I read in journals, I had also right away admired.

The years from '68 through the early 1970s—dates of our first meetings and the beginning of our friendship in thinking, in politics, in the university—marked for the three of us together and for each of us individually a significant turning point. It would call for long analyses which I cannot carry out here. As for me, after my position as assistant at the Sorbonne and then six years of teaching at ENS [the École Normale Supérieure] on the rue d'Ulm, after my first publications, there were already the beginnings of my irreversible break with the Tel Quel movement—not with the journal, of which I was never a part, but with the group, which put up less and less with my political independence with regard not only to their pro-PCF [Parti Communiste Français, the French Communist Party] and pro-Soviet positions in 1968 at the time of the invasion of Prague but, a bit later, with regard to their conversion, which was just as dogmatic, to a caricatural and blind Maoism accompanied by a somewhat childish intellectual terrorism. Those moments of solitude were difficult for me. From then on, Philippe and Jean-Luc's affectionate and hospitable complicity began in effect to turn Strasbourg, for me at least, into the symbol of a city of refuge. To this I should add that in the political reaction that followed 1968, in spite or because of the work the three of us were doing, and doing in a more and more visible way, in Strasbourg as well as in Paris, the powers that be of the university, represented by all sorts of administrative bodies, blocked us from professorship positions. This was for a long time the case for other philosophers among our friends, in particular Althusser, Rancière, and Sarah Kofman, our friend and ally from the beginning, whose memory I would like to pay tribute to here and of whom I will speak again in a moment. I must also say—though Philippe and Jean-Luc know this and would speak of it much better than I—that Lucien Braun's generous and protective presence will have done a great deal, on so many occasions, to make possible what our enemies wanted to forbid or shut away into a quasi-clandestineness.

The works of Philippe and Jean-Luc were more and more influential and celebrated, both here and elsewhere, for example, in Paris, and not only in Paris and not only among students. They began writing together texts that were remarkable and immediately remarked upon. This writing *à deux* would last for a number of years without preventing either of them from writing alone at the same time and, I imagine, writing alone even in their common works. This writing or thinking with two, three, or four hands has always been for me a fascinating, admirable, and enigmatic apparition, though still today just as unthinkable and impossible. Nothing seems to me more unimaginable, and I experience this as my own limitation—in a private life that was inseparable from the public experiences of which I am speaking—than their ties of familial community.

At the beginning of the 1970s, after having come to Strasbourg, I had the chance, in turn, to make Strasbourg—my Strasbourgian friends and hosts—come to Paris, first of all, and then to the United States. The globalization or worldwidization [*la mondialisation*], I would even say the other-worldwidization, of Strasbourgian philosophical thought was thus set in motion.

As for Paris, I will give just two or three examples. First, in 1970, after having met and reached an agreement with Michel Delorme, founder and director of the young Éditions Galilée—this faithful friend to whom the three of us owe so much, along with still others from Strasbourg, such as Daniel Payot, for example—after the publication of Philippe's and Jean-Luc's book on Lacan, a book that had a huge impact at the time and that Lacan himself, not without some grumbling, encouraged his followers to read and take into account, we founded, with Sarah Kofman, the collection "La philosophie en effet." With close to one hundred titles published, it is today, I dare underscore without any marketing intent, one of the most translated philosophy collections in the world, perhaps the most translated in the world for some of its works. It represents, I dare say again, a TGV—in the absence of any other[3]—a philosophical TGV between Paris and Strasbourg, transporting and transmitting everything that seemed to us exceptional and innovative in philosophy, and this without the least concern for promoting any school or doctrine. For, allow me to insist on this, there was never between the four of us, just as there was never between all those associated with us for one reason or another, any kind of doctrinal complicity, no common "line," and still less any homogeneity. Lines of division, differences, chiasms, borrowings (whether intentional or not), open and un-open debates, remained the rule of the day, and this was spontaneously accepted by everyone. Even in the books signed in common, differences in voice could be discerned without this ever becoming a sign of war, discord, or polemic. Now, of course, something must have brought us together, something that I would be unable to define here, especially in so little time. It would require long, thorough, and careful historico-philosophical analyses. Someday others perhaps will take an interest in doing this seriously. It will not be easy. But something must have facilitated our synagogue without synagogue, I dare not say our "community without community," which I would call, for lack of anything better, a respectful sense not only for the right to philosophy but for *justice* in thinking, which is also to say *probity* in writing, ethics, law, and politics. Jean-Luc has said and thought what had to be said and thought "of" probity (*Redlichkeit*) in one of his most beautiful texts, "Our Probity" ("*Unsere Redlichkeit*"). If I could mention, exceptionally, the title of one of my own books, *Politics of Friendship*, I would say that it owes almost everything, in its aims and in its aporias, to the experience that I have shared for thirty-five years with my friends from Strasbourg.

The second example of this shuttling back and forth, this TGV without TGV between Strasbourg and Paris, were the famous seminars given by Philippe and Jean-Luc at that ENS, where I was then teaching. These sessions on the retreat of the political brought together the most exacting thinkers and left deep traces in the political reflection of the times.

It was in those years—a third example—that I advised Yves Mabin (at the Ministry of Foreign Affairs), who had asked for my advice, to send my three friends, my three other musketeers of "La philosophie en effet," on a mission to the United States. This was the beginning of what I will pompously call our conquest of America. For since that time, all four of us have had multiple teaching engagements and conferences in the United States, from the East coast to—and especially—the West Coast: Strasbourg and Paris to Berkeley, San Diego, Irvine, though also Chicago, Buffalo, Baltimore, New York, and so many other places on every continent. With, from that time on, so many friends, colleagues, and students in common.

Let me pick up the pace so as not to keep you here too long. To stay in the 1970s, let me recall 1972, the first of our many ten-day conferences at Cerisy-la-Salle ("Nietzsche Today"), which was so significant that the thirtieth anniversary of this event was celebrated in Germany. Already the collusions of our synagogue without synagogue appeared to everyone as such, right out in the open, right before their eyes. Sarah, Philippe, Jean-Luc and I were all there, along with common friends like Lyotard and Deleuze, even though they were part of another "philosophical camp."

1974: another conference organized by Jean-Luc and Philippe that brought together right here all the friends and admirers of Roger Laporte.

1978: I travel from Basel to see Sophocles' *Antigone*, translated by Philippe Lacoue-Labarthe, who also directed it, along with Michel Deutsch, at the National Theater of Strasbourg. I first read the text on the plane, "aloud and yet just to myself," sometimes in German, sometimes in French. In a short and somewhat encrypted note that I wrote for the occasion under the title *"Ex abrupto,"* everything begins with a quotation: "Der Ort sagt . . . ," "The place says," "it is the place that dictates to me." Creon states: "Der Ort sagt mir wohl, was ich ordnen muss [It is the place that dictates to me what I must set in order]." Like Strasbourg today.

In *"Ex abrupto"* I make a somewhat veiled reference to a conversation on the benches of the theater with Claire on the subject of paternity and "impossible filiation." The last sentence then evoked a certain Hölderlin who "came to mingle with the crowd, a little lost, wondering no longer." Jean-Luc played a role in the play that he also performs with some talent in his family, that of a carpenter.

The years 1979–81 were for me among the richest of my Strasbourgeoisie. In May 1979, on my way to Freiburg-im-Breisgau, where I used the pretext of a lecture to let myself be haunted by Husserl and Heidegger, I stopped in Strasbourg and, as I recall in *The Post Card* (the project of which was beginning to take shape and whose "Envois" I would write the following summer), our friend Sam Weber, who was staying in Strasbourg, came to get me by car at the station to drive me to Freiburg. I confided in him as an absolute secret this project of *The Post Card*, and I realized when we got to Freiburg that he had already divulged the secret to one of our hosts there, Friedrich Kittler as it turned out, even before getting to Freiburg. The signatory of these fictive "Envois" recounts this story on the date May 9, 1979, and he announces all the conferences that awaited us, most notably in Strasbourg:

> I am writing you in the train that's taking me back from Strasbourg (I almost missed it, since it was S. accompanying me: he always arrives late, always the last [i.e., like Socrates, the subject of *The Post Card*]—when he arrives—there I was, waiting for him in Rue Charles-Grad where I had stopped over as I did on the way. We spoke about the Athenaeum [an allusion to the great book by Philippe and Jean-Luc, *The Literary Absolute*]—and about more than one symposium on the horizon: for we have to do it over, and several times in the year to come).[4]

All the symposia announced by this post card, which will mention them again, were so many hyphens and journeys between Strasbourg and other places, or better, trips and round trips to Strasbourg: Strasbourg, Paris, Strasbourg, Cerisy-la-Salle, Strasbourg, Grenoble, Strasbourg. First in May 1979, there was, in the Grand Amphithéâtre of the Sorbonne, with close to two thousand people in attendance, the Estates General of Philosophy, organized by GREPH,[5] in which Jean-Luc and Philippe were active participants from 1975 on, and not only by contributing to *Who's Afraid of Philosophy*? They were of course present at the Estates General and were among those most engaged. The following month there was, right here, the large international conference on "Le genre," organized by Philippe and Jean-Luc. It was one of their most remarkable successes in that genre of event. The following year, during the summer of 1980, there was first the Eighteenth Congress of the Sociétés de Philosophie de Langue Française on the theme of representation, organized by Lucien Braun and the University of Strasbourg. The opening address of the conference, which I delivered, was also entitled "Envoi," this time in the singular, as if the very gesture of sending—the "Envoi" of the lecture or the "Envois" of *The Post Card*—always had Strasbourg as its origin, destiny, or destination. That same summer, Philippe and Jean-Luc organized a ten-day conference at Cerisy-la-Salle under the title "The Ends of Man." In addition to the one that followed on Lyotard, this was the first in a series of such conferences at Cerisy in which just about all of us took part, in 1992, 1997, 2002. For that too I remain infinitely grateful to Jean-Luc and Philippe. From that conference of 1980, I will recall, for lack of time, just two things that are, should you be interested, archived in the seven hundred page volume published by Galilée that brings

together under the title *The Ends of Man* [*Les fins de l'homme*] the partici-
pation of nearly one hundred people in eighteen lectures and seven seminars. Two things, then. First, this was, at least as far as I can remember,
the first and only time in my life when, in the course of a conference
devoted to me, I came into conflict, and from the first day on, with a
couple of speakers about whom I had to ask Jean-Luc and Philippe why
in the world they had invited them (for I had nothing to do with the
organization of the conference, not in its choice of theme and not in the
selection of those invited). The future would prove me right: these two
speakers were soon to be the notorious authors of *La pensée 68*, and one
of the two has just recently had a stint, as brief as it was tragicomic, at
the Ministry of Education. The other, happier fact that I would like to
recall today, in order to recognize his presence, is that Jacob Rogozinski,
who was not yet Strasbourgeois, gave a beautiful talk entitled "Decon-
structing—the Revolution," a talk followed by a rich debate that is also
archived.

And then other beautiful Strasbourgeois voices came to be heard at
Cerisy, and this was the beginning of some great and precious friendships, with Rodolphe Burger and Isabelle Baladine Howald, who was, I
believe, the first person anywhere to speak so lucidly and so generously
of *The Post Card*, which had just been published.

1981: I will add two things to what Philippe and Jean-Luc recalled of
our trip at night and in the snow from Grenoble to Strasbourg, Philippe
at the wheel, and me preparing the dissertation defense of Mikkel Borch-
Jakobsen with a flashlight. The first is that, upon our arrival, we met up
with Levinas who said to me in an aside during the defense with a biting
and resigned irony: "Today, when one says the name God, one has to
add 'if you will allow me the expression!'" The other memory is that,
during this return to Strasbourg from the Cultural Center of Grenoble,
whose director was then Georges Lavaudant, we learned that a state of
war had just been declared by Wojciech Jaruzelski in Poland. This was
the beginning of a police crackdown in all the neighboring communist
countries. It was a week later, then, in this atmosphere of heightened
repression, that I was imprisoned in Prague on the absurd charges of
drug manufacturing and trafficking, though I had gone there to give
clandestine seminars organized by the Jan Hus Association, which had
just been founded by Jean-Pierre Vernant and myself. I always associate
that Prague adventure with this night-long trip between Grenoble and
Strasbourg.

I am speaking too much, as always. To accelerate my telegraphic narrative, and leaving aside all the theses and lectures that always led me back to Strasbourg, much more often than to any other French city, I will restrict myself, so to speak, to *parliamentary* things. After having participated in various Carrefours des littératures, overseen by Christian Salmon, Philippe, and Jean-Luc, always with the kind support of Catherine Trautmann, whom we will never thank enough for her help and advice, for the hospitality she so generously offered, first as mayor and then as minister of culture, I experienced, along with others, those great moments when, in the spirit of these Carrefours, we all took part in founding the International Parliament of Writers, alongside "personalities," as they are called, who are well known in the media: Pierre Bourdieu, Susan Sontag, Toni Morrison, Salman Rushdie, and so many others. This Parliament is today still very active, though under a new name, INCA, the International Network of Cities of Asylum. It continues to develop through publications and the designation of cities of asylum. I still take part in it in a more or less active way. But so as not to have to recount this history, already more than a decade long, a complex, international history, let me take refuge once again in a local anecdote. It was on the occasion of the arrival in Strasbourg for the International Parliament of Writers of the person who was to be its first president, Salman Rushdie, that I witnessed one of the funniest and most astonishing things in the life of a large city. The fact is that, in Strasbourg, the city's security services are able to change the name of a street for a single night, in order, for example—and this actually happened—to throw off potential assassins who might have tried to execute the *fatwa* pronounced by the Ayatollah Khomeni, the night when Salman Rushdie, surrounded by body guards, came to have dinner with us at a private residence in the city. I've forgotten the original and permanent name of the street, I've forgotten its substitute name or its name for a night, but I recall the surprise of my Strasbourgeois friends before the simulacrum of a brand new street sign whose name they did not recognize. The feared assassins could thus have known in what city, Strasbourg, in what *bourg* they were pursuing their victim, but they would have lost the trace of the evil and the *Strasse* of the crime they had premeditated. Strasbourg, I concluded, is a city that can change countries, a city that can change the name of its streets for a night, but the place name(d) [*le lieu dit*] Strasbourg remains and dictates Strasbourg: "Der Ort sagt . . ."

And then I don't want to forget the International College of Philosophy, which brought the three of us together from the beginning, in 1983, and of which Philippe, after me, and after Jean-François Lyotard, another Strasbourgeois by adoption, was for a time director. And then there were all the colloquia and ten-day conferences at Cerisy in which we all have participated over the last two decades, the conference on Lyotard, then the three following ones, organized and orchestrated by our dear common friend Marie-Louise Mallet, who will have shared so much with us, in GREPH, in the Estates General of Philosophy, in the College, in our collection "La philosophie en effet," where she published *La Musique en respect* (*Music Held in Respect*), and who admirably took charge of editing and publishing three Cerisy conferences, those of 1992 (*Le passage des frontières*), 1997 (*L'animal autobiographique*), and 2002 (*La démocratie à venir*). And then there were the two conferences on sovereignty at the Château de Castries and in Coimbra, Portugal, and then the conference on Jean-Luc at the International College of Philosophy, the proceedings of which have just been published, and then, and then . . .

One final parliamentary experience, the one that honored me most and of which I am almost as proud and grateful as I am here today: the speech against the death penalty that I was able to deliver in 2001 before the Council of Europe, upon the invitation of Emma Bonino, at a time when I was devoting a seminar of several years to this pressing subject and militating on many fronts or on behalf of many cases, in particular that of Mumia Abu Jamal.

Almost as proud and grateful as I am today, I said. And happy. What makes me today happier still, even more grateful and, moreover, confident in the future, is not only everything I have already received from all the friends and partners I have just recalled, and of course, in the first place, from the work as well as the friendship of Philippe and Jean-Luc, without whom none of this would have taken place and taken place in Strasbourg. The Rue Charles-Grad should one day bear their names. And even, I cannot help but dream, the university.

What makes me even more joyful and grateful today is especially, in the present and for the future, the feeling that, inaugurated in the university by Philippe, Jean-Luc, Lucien Braun, and others, and now rooted in the municipality under the enlightened guidance of Catherine Trautmann, these wonderful traditions seem to be resolutely and remarkably respected, assumed, developed. This is the case in the university and in the department of philosophy, notably by Gérard Bensussan and Jacob

Rogozinski (and I'm not forgetting the active role played by someone just passing through, like me, namely, Joseph Cohen), and it is also the case in the municipality thanks to the generous initiative of Mayor Fabienne Keller, of Robert Grossmann, President of the Urban Community of Strasbourg, of François Miclo, and all their associates.

To you all, from the bottom of my heart, the Strasbourgeois who I am at heart will always be grateful.

CHAPTER TWO

Discussion Between Jacques Derrida, Philippe Lacoue-Labarthe, and Jean-Luc Nancy
(2004)

JACQUES DERRIDA: Just a personal word of introduction before opening our discussion. First to tell you in my own name to what extent an
experience like today's remains and will remain precious, unique, and
inaugural. Sometimes at conferences one or two students get to partici-
pate, but the floor is usually reserved for the elders, that is, the professors
. . . Today, our conference has been given over entirely to students, who
are all doing remarkable work, who have offered up, each in his or her
own way, a series of provocative reflections. It's really quite unheard-of
and, in the end, unforgettable. It's a truly unique opportunity, something
extremely rare . . .

Second, thinking back to the session yesterday at the Kléber Bookstore
where someone asked the question of absence and presence, I remember
having said "sometimes those who are absent are more present than those
present," that is, sometimes living alongside someone is the best way, or
the worst way, of not paying attention to them and not noticing their
presence. Now at the moment when the three of us are appearing
together at the same table—and this too has rarely happened, maybe
never—*I was thinking to myself: this friendship that I hold so dear, like the
apple of my eye, if I had lived in Strasbourg, if I had seen them every day, I
don't know whether I would be here* . . . I think that a certain distance,
the "good distance" we spoke of yesterday, "the distance that is good [*la
distance bonne*]," has kept us and kept our friendship alive. And I'm

afraid of what's now going to happen. All right, so let me yield the floor right away, because I don't want to be the first to jeopardize . . .

PHILIPPE LACOUE-LABARTHE: First, if I understand correctly, it's best to remain a little absent, a bit distracted . . . We had agreed to bring to a conclusion both these three days and what took place here today: the four presentations we have just heard and then others that have been handed out, which, unfortunately, we will not be able to discuss because they were not presented. We had thus agreed to start from there and with a few lingering questions. In particular—I spoke of this very briefly with Jean-Luc in private—with regard to the final presentation and a certain impasse in *Being and Time* that is the result, in Heidegger, of both a *political decisionism* (a complicated and complex one at that, since the word *Entscheidung* does indeed mean *decision* in German—and especially in the German of the times, the German of Kantorowicz and of Jünger, the German of a certain extreme right, which one finds everywhere in Carl Schmitt, for example) and a certain impasse regarding the theme of the people. That's because if there is death, if there is sacrifice, if there is a "chosen death," that is, a death not only accepted but claimed, it is, as Kantorowicz puts it very well, "dying for one's country."

We thus wondered whether we wouldn't pick up things there in order to speak a bit of a theme that is common to Jacques and Jean-Luc, namely, *infinite finitude*. So I'm just throwing out these two questions to see what sense we can make of all this.

JEAN-LUC NANCY: I have to jump in here right away because you just said that the theme of *infinite finitude* is common to Jacques and Jean-Luc—but you're leaving yourself out . . .

PL-L: No, no . . .

J-LN: Yes, but with you it's *finite infinitude*.

JD: Okay, here we go . . .

PL-L: Yes, if you want . . .

J-LN: Yes, of course that's right!

PL-L: No, I didn't mean that . . . I meant that I never thematized it *like that*, and, moreover, I was never very receptive to it . . .

J-LN: I think there is something here, a certain *typology*, between the three of us. A typology in which you, Philippe, would be on the side of the *tragic*, Jacques on the side of the *undecidable*, and I . . . I don't know, maybe on the side of *anastasis* . . . And the way each of these three postures affects what is called *infinite finitude* is no doubt a real question.

But before getting into this, I would like to note that the last presentation we heard, which was very interesting and pertinent in its approach, ended by speaking of *Geschehen*. By ending with *Geschehen*, this presentation concluded its interpretation of section 65 of *Being and Time* by making as if, whether this was its intention or not, there were no reference some ten sections later to this sacrificial death for the people.[1] A death that has in fact the very remarkable characteristic of being the only death that assures *Dasein* access to *Geschick*, to *Geschehen* become *Geschick* and *Mitgeschick*, while—in what I find to be a very surprising way—just before acceding to the *Geschick*, we learn that *Dasein* exposed to its solitary death is "only"—I hope I am not the one introducing this "only" into the text, in any case, I have the impression that there is an at least implicit "only" in Heidegger's writing—"only" *Schicksalhaftigkeit*, that is, *being capable of . . ., being susceptible to receiving the blows of destiny*, of which its death is a part. But at that moment, we also learn that this *Schicksalhaftigkeit* is not yet *Geschicklichkeit*, which can take place only in death in battle for the people, the battle being itself for the cause of the people, and so on. Moreover, we find this sacrificial death later, in Heidegger's commentary on Hölderlin's *Germania*. There is here, it has to be said, something that must be thought and rethought. In any case, this cannot be done by holding in abeyance the whole affair that comes later or comes back later.

I don't want to say this like some kind of schoolmarm. As concerns the inheritance of Heidegger in Derrida, it is clear that the difference between solitary *Dasein* and *Dasein* in the *Volk* cannot but play an enormous role. And that's because, for you, there is no *Volk*. Not only is there nothing that resembles this problematic of the people, but you don't even want to use the word *people*. It's one of the words I use, but you—and you've told me this more than once—you don't even want to use it. Just like the word *community*. The same is true for Philippe, in fact. So from that point of view at least you two are on the same side.

But what I would then wish to add to all of this is the following. Leaving aside the political in the strict sense—even though there is obviously lots of politics, not Nazi politics, in 1927, but far right politics, particularly around this theme of the people and a "sacrificial death for the people"—it could be argued that what guided Heidegger up to this point in his thinking (and, once again, assuming we can separate off an ill-controlled *political habitus*, that is, as Philippe said earlier, one that remains in a passive attitude, that makes no real decision, that is content just to follow the prevailing current) was the only way he could find to extract the "death of *Dasein*" from this too possible or too certain impossibility, all the while being still unable to sense it or let it resonate in anything other than a purely negative way. What I mean is this: sensing that if he simply stayed with a *Dasein* isolated in its being toward death, the whole dimension of history, of the collective, and thus of *Geschehen*, of *Geschick*, would vanish, Heidegger, caught up in some sense by the path of his thought, would have been led to think the only possibility capable of propelling *Dasein* out of its existential solitude, that is, for Heidegger in 1927, a *sacrificial death for the people*. It would be necessary, obviously, to rethink all of this very carefully. But what I mean here is that if you, Jacques, by insisting on death as you do, by absolutely refusing to think it in any terms that might resemble a "sacrificial death" and thus by not inscribing it in any kind of collective destiny, I wonder if, in so doing, you don't nonetheless leave open the possibility of another operation, another apprehension, another "modified taking hold," as Heidegger says, the "modified taking hold" of *Uneigentlichkeit* [inauthenticity] that would make *Eigentlichkeit* [authenticity] of this same death. I mean that you always treat it in the same way, as you said earlier, namely, as that of which one must say nothing, of which one can say nothing . . . And one cannot but agree with you entirely on that. But, at the same time, does not what you call the *différance* of the instant in the instant and *différance* in general, and thus the finite character of infinitude (this brings us back to Philippe's question) make it necessary to think the unthinkable, to think precisely there where one cannot think, namely, that there is something at stake that would have to be distinguished from a dialectical sublation? Something that would have to be distinguished from every kind of resurrection—so, you see, at this point I am willing to sacrifice any *anastasis*. And this something would have to be distinguished from any tragic possibility, which is really the possibility of still saying something on the basis of . . ., of still doing something with it . . . It is the possibility by which philosophy passes into poetry, as Philippe would say. And so, Jacques, is there something for you, at this point, a possibility, or is there nothing?

JD: I don't know. I find it difficult to answer your question in this form. But let me say two things that will perhaps go in the direction of what you are asking me . . . The first remark is that, for Heidegger, *Dasein* is, let's not forget it, indissociable from *Mitdasein*, from *Mitsein*. Indissociable: it's one and the same breath; it's two breaths that cannot be dissociated. The question that then arises is the following: How does one dissociate *sterben*, the dying of *Dasein*, which is alone in its capacity for authentic being and which is thus, implicitly, the individual, the individual *Dasein*, from what Montaigne would call *comourance* [co-dying]? *Co-mourants* are those who die together, lovers who want to die together. Those who die together and those who die collectively for some cause or other. I don't know how to treat Heidegger's discourse on being toward death, his whole description, and then the indissociability of *Dasein* and *Mitsein*, and thus the death of the other, whether simultaneous or not, with the problematic of mourning . . . I just don't know. What is death for *Mitsein*, not to mention for the *Volk*?

J-LN: But that's just it. It seems to me that what Heidegger says of "the sacrificial death for the sake of the people" answers this question without compromising the solitude of *Dasein* . . . Because it's precisely not a *co-mourance*, as you put it, as Montaigne puts it, because the co- is in some sense dissolved and subsumed in the *Volk*. That is, *Volk* is community, but there's a part of it that is public, common . . .

JD: But then why—and this is an enormous, eminently political question—why determine *Mitsein* as *people*?

PL-L: In fact, there's not just the *people*. I am going to say something very simple that informed readers of Heidegger know: there is not only the *Volk*, there is also, to determine *Mitsein*, the word *generation*. A same generation . . . that of Jean-Luc and me, and that of Jacques, well, there's a difference. This has always been for me an enigma, namely, that Heidegger can think in terms of *generation* . . . Or else, in a very crude way, one would have to apply this term to age groupings or classes—drafts—in an almost "tactico-military" sense of the term: the class of 1960, the class of 1970. This generation might then be related to the word that was used in military campaigns, German as well as French, to designate people of the same "generation": "conscripts." This word *conscript* was used to refer to "conscription," that is, to people of the same age . . .

J-LN: . . . and "conscription" is "co-inscription" . . .

PL-L: It's "co-inscription," yes, that's what I meant . . .

JD: But we are obviously not going to be able to think this problematic on the basis of a general mobilization. Especially since the word *generation* is one of the words that has always seemed untenable to me: *we don't know what a generation is.* Who is of the same generation? Let me tell you an anecdote. Recently *La Quinzaine Littéraire* asked a number of people, including me, to respond to the question "Who do you think you are [*pour qui vous prenez-vous*]?" and I had the gumption to try to respond. I responded with the title "Survivre, sursaut, sursis" ("Survival, surprise, suspension"). At a certain moment in this text, I said that we are all survivors in reprieve [*en sursis*]. Some perhaps a little more than others—me, for example, because of what is called age, illness, and so on. And so I accept being called a *survivor*—as they often write in the newspapers. But what I won't accept is being called the "last survivor" of a "generation" of philosophers, thinkers, writers, who are all dead: Barthes, Deleuze, Foucault, and so on. As if I belonged to the same "generation" or as if we belonged to the same grouping. I find this revolting, not only because of the question of age—since I am, it has to be said, the youngest of this "generation"—but also and especially because it is not a "generation." Obviously, we have things in common, but there is no "generation." I thus hate it when one says that I am the "survivor of the generation of the thinkers of '68." And the same is true between Philippe, Jean-Luc, and myself; there is a difference in age, among other things, that prevents us from being of the same "generation." We are not of the same "generation." They could have been my students. I have students who are now sixty years old . . .

J-LN: You were a lecturer [*assistant*] at the Sorbonne when I was a student. But I never had any contact with you, I don't know why . . .

JD: Good thing, too! In any case, the concept of "generation" has no philosophical meaning [*sens*]. It can have a kind of demographic or sociological meaning, but it has no philosophical meaning. The second remark I would like to make—here again, without knowing whether I am answering the question—is that I have a theory about responses. Well, if not a theory, a quip . . . It's that, in responding to someone, whenever one responds well, in a just fashion, to the question asked, it's of absolutely no interest; it's a programmed response, an expected response, in short. To respond in a just fashion, one has to respond *a bit off topic*, a bit to the side. Not just to any side, but *just to the side*. And so in order to respond just to the side, I would say that, unfortunately for me, what I said about mourning, about death, is terrible. These are totally despairing thoughts, but, in the end, they have to be thought. For death obliges us to think. In facing death, we are *obliged* to think *this* [ça]. We can go into a cemetery, stand before the casket of someone we loved, and cry . . . but we know that there is *nothing*, that nothing comes back or redounds to the other, and that, in the end, all we can do is keep silent . . . But then, on the contrary, in my anticipation of death, in my relation to a death to come, which I know will annihilate me, obliterate me completely, there is, beneath the surface, testamentary desire, that is, the desire that *something* survive, be left behind, transmitted—an inheritance or something to which I myself do not aspire, that will not come back to me, that I will not receive, but that, perhaps, will remain . . . And this [ça] is a feeling that haunts me not only for what are called works and books, but for every banal, everyday gesture that will have been witness to *this* and that will keep the memory of *this* when I will no longer be there. Now I said that this was a part not of death, of the impossible experience of death, but of *my* anticipation of death. And so, for me, this has always taken on an obsessive character, one that concerns not only, once again, things that are in the public domain, writing, but even private things . . . I always ask myself whenever I leave a piece of paper at home or write something in the margins of a book—an exclamation mark, for example—*Who is going to read this?* And *what will my children get from this, if they ever read this?* Or again, about fifty years ago, when I borrowed from the library at the École Normale Supérieure Heidegger's *Kant and the Problem of Metaphysics*, I—this is a bad habit of mine that horrifies my sons—scribbled some things in the margins of that book . . . And I found that book again one day when I returned to the École. And all of a sudden I saw things that I had written fifty years earlier in the margins of the *Kantbuch*. And so people are going to come along one day and ask: *What is this? Who did this? This is what?* Those kinds of thoughts, what I call testamentary thoughts, which I have tried to link to the structure of the trace—all traces are of a testamentary essence[2]—have always haunted me. Even if it does not take place, even if it is not received, there is a testamentary desire that is part of the experience of death . . . But I don't know if I've responded to your question.

J-LN: You've responded perfectly well. I would like, however, to add an additional aspect to the question. Namely, in the word *exappropriation*, I often, most often, have the impression that what one hears being accentuated is only the *ex–*, as if it were simply the doublet of *expropriation*. But, since you created the word *exappropriation*, it's clearly not just *expropriation* that you are thinking about but also *propriation*. So what you just said is, I think, in line with this *propriation*. That, in the end, is all that matters to me. For I think that, for you, there is a proper, a *propriation* ever more buried, ever more abyssal, ever more impossible, and, at the same time, possible in this impossibility. It is not simply the expropriation of an activity . . .

JD: What I wished to say with *exappropriation* is that in the gesture of appropriating something for oneself, and thus of being able to keep in one's name, to mark with one's name, to leave in one's name, as a testament or an inheritance, one must expropriate this thing, separate oneself from it. This is what one does when one writes, when one publishes, when one releases something into the public sphere. One separates oneself from it and it lives, so to speak, without us. And thus in order to be able to claim a work, a book, a work of art, or anything else, a political act, a piece of legislation, or any other initiative, in order to appropriate it for oneself, in order to assign it to someone, one has to lose it, abandon it, expropriate it. That is the condition of this terrible ruse: we have to lose what we want to keep and we can keep only on the condition of losing. It's very painful. The very fact of publishing is painful. It departs, one knows not where, it bears one's name, and—it's horrible—one is no longer even capable of reconstituting it oneself, not even of reading it. That's *exappropriation*, and it applies not only to those things we speak of with relative ease, that is, literary or philosophical works, but to everything, to capital, to the economy in general.

PL-L: I am haunted by this same thing, I have this same—I'm no longer sure what to call it—testamentary or testimonial haunting. For a very long time now, through things read long ago, a very strong feeling has been inscribed, so to speak, in me: that of leaving something, a trace, and, in the end, to *transmit* . . . It is something that struck me in the

declaration of someone I like a great deal, and it was considered scandal-
ous by . . . precisely not by you two. It's a declaration of Malraux's. He
said: "My ambition was to leave a trace somewhere." And he did not say
what kind of trace. I know, however, that there is a very powerful con-
nection here with the anticipation of death, being haunted by death. So
I know very well what you mean. I recognize something in what you are
saying, as is so often the case. But at the same time, this haunting—and
this is to respond to Jean-Luc—can have the appearance of *conservation*.
One keeps something—I'm right now in the process of moving, I know
what it means to have kept tons of things. I keep, I keep, I have all kinds
of things in closets, in the bottom of drawers . . . It can be something
completely insignificant, but I cannot refrain from keeping, from con-
serving, and it's not in order to appropriate it for myself. Absolutely not.
I realize this in an exemplary way: this does not belong to me, this no
longer belongs to me. It's there, it's put in reserve, and I don't even know
for whom it might be destined. It is, so speak, without a proper *telos*.

J-LN: First, let me say, just to confirm what you are saying: I once
threw away all the letters I had been keeping . . .

JD: Really . . .

J-LN: . . . but you'll see, I regretted it. It was when I was about thirty,
maybe thirty-five. It was piling up, it was monstrous, and then I tried to
archive, to number things, to classify them . . . This was before knowing
you, maybe just before. And so one day I got rid of it all, telling myself
that it was useless, that it served no purpose . . . But very soon therefore
I deeply regretted it. And now, like you, I don't throw anything away
either. Nothing, I mean nothing. Useless pieces of paper, batteries, choc-
olates . . . and I don't know what to do with it all! . . . Now, if this were
a "TV talk show" I would ask you: How do you both understand Spinoza's line "We feel and know by experience that we are immortal"?

JD: For me, Spinoza is someone I have never understood at all. I have
taught him, I know something about him, I can give a course on Spinoza.
But—even though he was a Portuguese Marrano, like myself—he is a
thinker whose philosophical enterprise is to me the most "foreign." And
so, *to know by experience that I am immortal*, that . . . I recall having
spoken about this once with a friend, someone all three of us know, in

fact. I said to him that, in the end, naturally, I don't believe in immortality. But I know that there is an *I*, a *me*, a living being who is related to itself through autoaffection, who might be a bird and who will feel alive like me, and who might thus say, in silence, *me*, and who will be *me*! There will be some living being who will continue to say me and this will be a me, this will be me! I could give other examples. But I don't take much comfort in this.

J-LN: Spinoza's immortality . . .

JD: Maybe. When I am dead, there will be a bird, an ant, who will say "me" for me, and when someone says "me" for me, that's me. But just to pick up on what the two of you were saying about your papers, I once destroyed a correspondence. With a fierce determination: I tried to reduce it to shreds—it didn't work; I burnt it—that didn't work . . . I destroyed a correspondence I should not have destroyed and I will regret it for the rest of my life. As for the rest—and here we are speaking of the problem of the archive—I've never lost or destroyed anything. Right down to the little notes that Bourdieu or Balibar would leave on my door when I was a student saying "I'll come by later" . . . Or from Bourdieu, "I'll give you a call," and I still have these things—I have *everything*. The most important things and the most apparently insignificant things. Always hoping, of course, that one day—not thanks to immortality but thanks to longevity—I might be able to reread, to recall, to revisit, and, in some way, to reappropriate all of this for myself. And then I had the cruel and bitter experience—now that all of this correspondence has been archived and filed away, for the most part outside my home—that unfortunately I will never reread these things . . . Sometimes they send me a letter from my family when the signatory has to be identified, and so I reread that letter, but that is just one out of a hundred or a thousand! And so I know that what I kept is, for me, absolutely lost, though I kept this not for others but also for myself, in order to recall, and thus keep my experience, my memory, my past . . . That's *exappropriation*: I wanted to keep everything in order to appropriate for myself, but in order to keep and appropriate it, it was first of all necessary to put it in a *safe* place [*safe* in English in original]. And when one puts something in a safe place, it has to be elsewhere, elsewhere than on oneself. And the safe place is always the least safe place; it is always the place where something is objectified, conserved outside, and thus in the end not safe or protected from anything at all. For example, a part of my archives is in a place in the United States where there are earthquakes every ten years and another part is in some miserable shack where there could be a fire. And so there is no shelter, and I am bereft of the very thing I wanted to keep.

Just one more word about testaments, generations, and filiations: the day I decided to entrust these archives to the outside, it was not only because I had been asked to do so (the archives include all my seminars, lectures, and so on), but also because I came to realize that my children would not be able to publish, to concern themselves with, to take on the responsibility of, these archives. I came to realize that, at home—how can I say this without accusing anyone?—everything might be well preserved in the sense of material security but there would not be, so to speak, any readers. Elsewhere, however, there might be readers of certain seminars, of some of my correspondence—there are many insignificant exchanges of letters and then there are some that might be of interest to some people . . . But when I recognized—for reasons that I accept and that are understandable—that my sons would not be able to be develop an interest in all these things, I said to myself at that moment that it's better to give it all away.

PL-L: Let me respond just to the question posed by Jean-Luc—since this has turned into a TV talk show: "What do you think of Spinoza's line?" Okay, I too have a very complicated relationship with Spinoza, as well as with those who claim to follow him. This line has always touched me very deeply, even though the one philosophical phrase that really irks me is the one we have inherited, as you know, from antiquity, that of the immortality of the soul. To be very crude here, it's a load of metaphysical bullshit. It means nothing. Yet "we feel and know by experience that we are immortal"—that can happen. It happens. And I say this without wanting to explain it; I say it because it has happened to me. It has happened to me—now that we are revealing secrets—in the experience of love, and in a dazzling way. But I am persuaded it can happen in other ways. If I had such a shock when I received the last writing of Blanchot, *The Instant of My Death*, it was because, all of a sudden, I recognized this in that title and in that text, even if it remains very enigmatic—and Jacques knows this better than I do. I recognized in what Blanchot calls *the instant of my death* this experience of immortality. I would be interested today not to recount this but to formulate it.

JD: Just a word, Jean-Luc, to complicate a bit what I said about immortality. It is true that, in the Spinozistic sense, I never feel immortal. That being said, in the sense in which Freud says that no one believes in his or her own death, that even when one is obsessed with being followed at every instant by mortality, there is something here that I cannot believe. In this sense, I feel immortal, in my naïve and unconscious belief—the unconscious does not know death—and so I say, yes, in this sense, I feel something like: "I cannot die!" But this does not contradict the certainty that, one day, I am going to die.

J-LN: No, there isn't any contradiction, especially since Freud speaks precisely of a *belief.* I thus cannot believe because I cannot subscribe to a supposed or presupposed knowledge which I know at the same time cannot become a knowledge for me. In this sense, the statement "I believe that I am not going to die!" would mean that I subscribe immediately, spontaneously, and indefinitely to the most elementary feeling of my own existence. And so long as I live, I cannot but subscribe to this feeling, and even a second before dying, I subscribe to it still. That is the way I understand Freud. But it seems to me that Spinoza is speaking of something else. He speaks of a *feeling* and of a *knowing by experience.* I don't know if you hear it in this way, but I would say: I feel it and experience it as the *feeling* and *experiencing* of the limit of all feeling and all experiencing. As a result, this is neither a belief nor a non-belief—it's situated elsewhere. Perhaps this communicates with something else that could no longer be called faith. But, in any case, something that would first be of the order of affect, of affect at the limit of all possible affection, at the very limit of *being-affected.* And I would say to you this evening that I have the very strong impression that you are situated precisely at this limit and that, at the same time, you push it away. And so you too begin to insist on *exappropriation.* In your response, you insisted on loss. "To keep, one must lose." There, I would say, it's a question of tone, of accent. You, of course, accentuate "one must lose." I'm not asking you to accentuate "to keep." I am not trying to get you to admit that, in the end, you reappropriate everything for yourself. But it's simply this: we are coming close to something that Heidegger wanted to name with the triplet *Er-eignis, Ent-eignis, Zu-eignis.* That is to say, the appropriating event, which is the de-propriating event, which is also—we might say—the *deviant* or deliquating event.

I would like to ask you another question, if you don't mind. A question that you can answer very quickly. It's something else entirely, but since you spoke of the bird that you will become, I would nonetheless like to know . . .

JD: What kind?

J-LN: Well, you didn't specify. If you want, we can decide . . . How about a humming bird? One has to be kind . . .

No, earlier, you spoke many times in favor of animals and against "the animal without world." ³ You insist on the fact that there are animals that mourn, and so on. Earlier you gave us a very impressive list. You talked about everything: love, work, speech. But in doing this, it seems to me that you are nonetheless *reestablishing* a scale, for you made it quite clear that the ant, for example, is not the same thing as the chimpanzee . . .

JD: It's not a scale, it's a difference . . .

J-LN: A difference. But what I wanted to ask you in the end is whether, by blurring the difference between the human and all other living beings, you don't end up reestablishing a difference?

JD: I never wanted to blur the difference between what is called the human and the animal. I wanted to call into question the linear and oppositional limit between the human and the animal in order, on the contrary, to introduce a greater differentiation. I am not so asinine [*bête*] as to think that the dog is just as much a philosopher as Heidegger. No, I know that there is a difference, that there are many differences, between humans and between humans and animals. My discourse is thus not against difference; it's against the oppositional limit that would mark out, on one side of the border, the possibility of speech, laughter, economy, clothing, tears, mourning, death—the animal does not die for Heidegger—and, on the other side, neither "as such" nor mourning nor signification nor response . . . This word *response* is the operative term here from Descartes to Lacan. The animal can signify, but its significations are *reactions* and never *responses*. Both Descartes and Lacan say this: the animal does not have access to the signifier because it cannot *respond*. It can only *react*. On this point, Lacan is profoundly Cartesian. That is what I contest. I don't contest this in order to say that the animal can *also* respond like the human can. I contest the certainty that the human can respond without reacting, or that the human's response is a pure response without reaction. There is some reaction in every response . . . And so, you see, I find that the concept no longer holds, no longer holds up . . .[4]

CHAPTER THREE

Opening
(2003)

JACQUES DERRIDA: Since I didn't know whether I would be able to be with you here today, and especially whether I would be able to deliver a real talk, I decided, with François Noudelmann, whom I would like to thank for his generosity in granting me complete freedom, to leave things up in the air until the last minute and to provide no title for what should be on my part a simple show of solidarity and symbolic friendship for a College whose existence has been dear to my heart since its birth some twenty years ago. "Opening" ("Ouverture") is thus the vague or false title that we had left as open and, precisely, as opening as possible.

But if I were to choose a more precise title today, now that I am here, I would borrow while imitating—with all requisite insolence, presumption, impertinence, and foolhardiness, and thus, by the same token, all necessary modesty and circumspection—that of the great little text of Kant, "*Was ist Aufklärung?*" ("What is Enlightenment?"). What, then, would our College have to do with, what will it have had to do with, the Enlightenment of today or tomorrow? What will it have had to think or rethink about it? But, of course, I will not say anything that might live up to this title. I'm just playfully suggesting a direction for a re-elaboration of this question. Another possible title, since I will be speaking of genesis and, especially, of generation, would have been, and you can hear it as you please: "The first of the generations of the International College of Philosophy."

To tell you the truth, I will speak for just a few minutes, in order to open this session and the discussion to follow, long enough to give or, as we say, to *pass over* the floor to Jean-Luc Nancy. I will thus be but a passer [*passeur*],[1] and I wonder, in light of the title of the paper to follow ("Que s'est-il passé?"; "What Came to Pass?"), whether the College was not, in its own way, the instituting of a certain passage, hospitality offered by passers or passers-by to other passers or passers-by, thereby forming a community without community that would be as inoperative as it is working, as declared as it is clandestine and unavowable.

Those who inaugurated the College laid down at the outset the principle that its members would not hold any place or position in a permanent and statutory way but would simply pass through, both in the sense of the passer who effaces him or herself in his or her research and teaching (whether scientific, philosophical, artistic, or literary) and in the sense of the passer-by who, having come to a seminar with no particular status, retains the right to speech and to critique.

But I suspect that this is not the most obvious meaning of Jean-Luc Nancy's title "What Came to Pass?" The phrase gestures instead, I imagine, toward the event, toward events, the philosophical and political history that preceded and followed the foundation of the International College of Philosophy, rather than toward the *passing* of the passage, of the passers and passers-by. It remains to be asked what *to pass* and what *having come to pass* mean in general. And why the French expression *se passer* ("come to pass") and *se passer de* ("pass up on") are so resistant to translation. An anniversary is not the worst moment to insist on such a question. But I said I wanted to be brief.

Allow me first of all to say straightaway and straightforwardly: I am very happy, truly, that the College is twenty years old and that I've been given the opportunity, the chance, to take part in the festivities and in the celebration of this event, and, more modestly, in reflections upon *what came to pass*, as it is put in the title chosen by Jean-Luc Nancy, and in the projections, hopes, and resolutions that this anniversary elicits for the future.

The College "Twenty Years After," therefore, though I shall resist the temptation to recount its history, intrigue, or drama against the backdrop of *The Three Musketeers*, *Twenty Years After*, and *The Vicomte of Bragelonne*, which I've just finished rereading, with great enthusiasm as a great book and, among other things, a great history lesson and lesson in political philosophy regarding the relationship between civil society and the sovereignty of the state, the secret and public space, and so on.

Back in the day when this singular counter-institution was founded by three, four, or five musketeers or *franc-tireurs* ("free-shooters"), I was certainly not the only one to think that, given the precariousness and fragility, given all the uncertainties that were threatening and were already perceptible, given all the opposition from political as well as university places, the College would not have the strength to confront all of this and so would not live for twenty years, maybe not even ten, maybe not even three or four. I was not the only one to doubt that it would live or survive for the time of a *generation* (and twenty years is more or less a generation), a philosophical and political generation. And in the end it is of generation and its contrary, the risk of death or degeneration, that we should perhaps speak this morning, without forgetting that, however enigmatic the expression *generation* and *philosophical generation* may be, something that lasts for some twenty years, the College has always been, from the beginning, the place of more than one generation, and it remains an institution where generations do not follow upon one another but cross, cohabit, share, or do not share the same training and the same philosophical memory. I was thus not the only one to doubt, though I hesitated to say so, that our College would live or survive the time of a generation. Such a length of time seemed to us, seemed to me, to me especially, highly unlikely. I am happy today to have been wrong and to be able to thank all those who have contributed to this life and this survival; this is a gratitude that I allow myself to express in the name of all those who formed, twenty years ago, the first College Assembly.

Of course it might be said—not to rain on this parade—that we still have not broached the question of whether it really has survived for twenty years, whether it has done better than just survive, whether it has been steadily degenerating or has been kept alive through extraordinary measures. And so the question is whether it is indeed the same College, the College of which we dreamt, which we had projected and which, of course, did not have to remain the same, whether it is indeed the same College that has lasted or passed the time of a generation. One would hope both "yes" and "no," that it has remained faithful to something like the heritage of a constitution or founding charter and that, at the same time, as this charter laid out, it has changed, it has invented, it has constantly reinvented itself, sometimes on the verge and at the risk of betrayal. One must always try to know what price is being paid for duration and what the limits are of acceptable concessions, compromises, or compromises of principle. In other words, one must know what is a good and what is a bad betrayal of a commitment [*engagement*]. One must always try to know this, though one never knows it in the form of a present and determinate judgment. One must speak in the future perfect, and even then I'm not sure, and for essential reasons, that one day we will be able to say, in all objective and theoretical certainty, in the future perfect: the College *will have been* a success. Without untangling this skein of questions, to which we shall surely return, I am nonetheless sure that it is right to acknowledge a certain success, a success that is certain. The College is solidly enough established; it is recognized, just enough legitimated and just enough illegitimate, just as we had wished, at once strong and fragile, visible and desirable or enviable in a national and international space. With a politics oriented toward high school teachers and toward all the "untitled" and "undocumented" workers of academe, with its public events, seminars, publications, radio shows, and its Saturday "book forums" (which I consider to be the most valuable, the most original, indeed the most unique opportunity of this kind for reading and opening discussions that take place nowhere else, not in the university and not in the press, where one speaks so little, except on very rare exceptions, of the kinds of books that matter to us. In the end, that is perhaps the rule that has been economically and telegraphically formulated by the College, its watchword and the slogan of its Enlightenment, of its counter-models for a new public space. This slogan would say: not like the majority of the press, not like the culture of the media, not like the vast majority of the university, but something else and something better than that in order to make up for the serious failings, the politically and philosophically serious failings, of all these things). In conjunction with all of this, internationality will have been one of the most remarkable features of this success, even if there remains much to be done in this area, as in others. The fact that this session is being chaired by my dear friend Natalia Avtonomova, whom I met at the Academy of Science of Moscow in the early 1990s and who has continued to be an indefatigable, indispensable, and lucid mediator between France, the USSR, and Russia—first of all through her own work and translations—is one of the proofs of the very real internationality of the College. It is also an indication that sexual difference will have been, I would venture to say, treated at the College better than elsewhere, as was in fact the recommendation of the *Rapport bleu*.[2] This was the case right from the start, and there are still a certain number of us here who can attest to it. Let me recall in passing that the most continuous seminar, the one that will have marked and lasted the entire life of the College (notably in its privileged and important association with the University of Paris VIII and in particular its doctoral program in feminist studies), will have been the one that Hélène Cixous has devoted to an "Analytics and Poetics of Sexual Difference." We must thus thank and congratulate those who, in one place or in another, have contributed to all of this, with a special token of gratitude today for the current College and for François Noudelmann, who has taken the initiative for and organized so well these days of public celebration, though also of work, artistic performances, and candid reflection on what happened or came to pass, what did not happen or come to pass, and what should or must from now on come to pass. I am in no way entitled to be the first to speak here, even less to dole out praises and criticisms. If I were entitled in any way, it would be precisely in the name of the *passé*, which is to be understood not so much in the sense given it by Jean-Luc Nancy, that of the event and of the transformation of the College in a generation within a historical and philosophico-political landscape that would itself call for long and difficult analyses, but simply in the name of the "passed," and so less in the name of the past as what *came to* pass [*ce qui s'est passé*] than in the name of what *has* passed or what *is* passed (even though lots of things came to pass at the origin of the College). I imagine that I was today given the honor of being the first to speak in the name of the old days or days of yore, perhaps even the archaic, I won't go so far as to say the *archē* of the College. But it so happens that in spite or because of my nostalgia or my seniority I have no desire to speak, at least not spontaneously, of origins. Of these origins, of this genealogy or this archeology, I will thus say nothing, except to note that if the founding of the International College of Philosophy will have been an event, the premises for it go back long before the time when Mitterrand came to power and a new political situation was able to help things along. The premises of the College go back at least as far as the theoretical and philosophical advances of the 1960s, back to May 1968, back to the founding and work of GREPH in 1974 and the Estates General called by GREPH in June 1979 that saw such massive turnout. If any of you wish, I would be happy during the discussion period to try to recount or describe in a more concrete and even anecdotal way what happened or came to pass during the very first years of the College and even during the year that prepared its founding. These origins have their archive, a no doubt partial and incomplete archive, selective as well, if only in the form of this little book, *Le rapport bleu*, which bears the subtitle "The Historical and Theoretical Sources of the International College of Philosophy." I recommend not just reading but vigilantly decoding it to anyone who wants to get a better sense of the shared vision, yes, but also of the entire virtual *dissensus* that already gathered together, so to speak, the first passers of the College. It seems to me that the College has for the most part held to the spirit and sometimes the letter of what is written in the first two parts of this *Rapport* ("The Regulative Idea" and "The Constitution"). It has done so through numerous adjustments and in response to pressures of various kinds, all the while taking into account the lessons drawn from experience as well as the idioms and idiosyncrasies of each of us. As for the part entitled "Projections," where each of the musketeers (Châtelet, Faye, Lecourt, and myself) signed individually his contribution and his philosophical desire, the virtual or manifest forms of *dissensus* that could already be read there have continued to develop and intensify over the course of these twenty years, and, in the end, this is a good thing.

Having said that, I wish to acknowledge without further delay, in order to pay them the great homage they deserve, the memory of my friends François Châtelet and Jean-François Lyotard. Both of them, each in his own way, have left an ineffaceable mark on this place. It was at the home of François Châtelet, who was already sick, that we often met in order to prepare the so-called *Rapport bleu*, whose first aim, as part of the mission I was charged with coordinating, was to prepare and justify the founding of the College. There we were, the four of us (four musketeers trying to outwit political sovereignty, working between the head of state and one of his ministers, who was, to be sure, our ally in principle, and already fighting on an almost daily basis against certain political and economic powers so as to preserve a freedom that we wished to be unconditional). During those meetings the four of us worked together, François Châtelet, Jean-Pierre Faye, Dominique Lecourt, and myself. Jean-François Lyotard soon joined us in an unofficial capacity and participated with fervor and vigilance in this preparatory reflection. Like the four of us who had been given responsibility for the project, he took part in the first College Assembly, then replaced me already in the second year in the position of Director, when I felt I had to resign in order to protect the time and energy needed for my own work from the crushing administrative responsibilities that fell on the one who was then called the Director and whom you now call today the President of the College Assembly. I remained affiliated with the College for some fifteen years, up until my resignation from the Scientific Council, a fact I recall only in order to explain why I feel totally incapable of judging from the inside the work of the College. I will thus refrain from doing so, having on this subject only indirect, empirical, and not easily formalizable impressions—and very contradictory ones as well, sometimes admiring and sometimes, shall we say, worrying.

The College is thus twenty years old, and it is celebrating these twenty years. One might say: longevity is good, but it is not a virtue in and of itself, and it is not the surest sign of health or of some fidelity to oneself, to one's origins, or to some originary project. It can sometimes cost one dearly; indeed, it can even come at the cost of longevity itself. The College, for example, has today reached the age that at one time marked the passage from minority to majority, or else, as Kant would put it, the age of the passage to Enlightenment. In *Was ist Aufklärung?* Kant begins, as you all recall, by defining Enlightenment as an age, as an exiting (*Ausgang*), as man's exiting from a minority (*Unmündigkeit*) in order to accede to a majority (*Mündigkeit*, a majority which also has the sense of emancipation). Majority, twenty years, is thus, if you will, the age of the emancipated majority, that is to say, the capacity for independent judgment, that which is precisely lacking in the minor, the force to make use freely and independently of one's understanding without any need of direction from any board of education, from the teaching, authority, or institutional tutelage of some other person. But even if one is not satisfied, as would be my case, with this interpretation of the Enlightenment—about which, rest assured, I am not about to subject you to a lecture—what is remarkable and paradoxical in the beginning of this text is that the non-majority, immaturity, minority (*Unmündigkeit*) is not interpreted, as one would be tempted to think, and Kant insists on this a great deal, as some kind of innocence or irresponsibility. Minority without maturity remains responsible and accountable, even culpable for itself (*aus seiner selbstverschuldeten Unmündigkeit*). Because it stems less from a weakness of understanding than from a lack of daring and courage. *Sapere aude!* Dare to know: that is the motto of the Enlightenment for those who have come of age. There is a lesson to be drawn from this important passage, in a text that also concerns, as you know, freedom, public space, and institutions, the institutions that Kant claimed to be, like "formulas" (*Satzungen und Formeln*), the mechanical tools (*mechanischen Werkzeuge*) of a rational employment or rather misemployment of one's natural gifts, like the little shackle bells or chimes that one attaches to the feet (*Fußschellen*) of a minority when it persists in its being, when it insists on remaining minor, when immaturity is bent on lasting, bent on its longevity as minority, as immaturity responsible for its immaturity. There is thus a fetishization of the institution; it is as if responsible immaturity found in the institution the shoe that fits it (and you know that the shoe and the foot are important examples of everything that lends itself to fetishization). And so the somewhat allegorical lesson that I would like to draw from this passage is that, if the College was not, at the origin, of age, if it wanted to have the appearance of a minority in its minority, this stemmed neither from an originary and insignificant innocence nor from a simple irresponsibility cloaked in some institutional mechanism but from the fact that the foundation of the College, and then its entire history, gained their meaning and drew their possibility as well as their responsibility not only from the state of a French and then global political and philosophical situation but from a veritable battleground, full of old roots and new shoots, in France and abroad. And it is this network of multiple and overdetermined conflicts, from the 1960s to the end of the 1970s and from the early 1980s right up to 2003, that must be questioned, analyzed, reflected upon ceaselessly and uncompromisingly in order to understand what happened, what came to pass, and what might, what will be able to, or what ought to come to pass in the future of the College, in the name of the College, or in the name of everything for which the College is also, let us never forget, one symptom among others.

Having lived through this time, having belonged to it, I, like all of you, have accumulated a certain number of signs, memories, interpretations, and perspectives on this subject, all partial in both senses of the term, since I was part of this group and took sides in all of these wars, in the College and outside the College. But for that very reason, I would be incapable today, and not only for lack of time, of offering you a general, neutral, and formalized reading of this battlefield, of the great or small quakes that transformed its geography, in France and in the world. Perhaps in the discussion to follow I will venture to say something about this by sharing some past experiences and some possible interpretations.

Having thus expressed my admiration and gratitude to our hosts of the current College, it is time for me to give the floor over to Jean-Luc Nancy, who was from the beginning and remains today, in his person and in his work, one of the most exemplary actors, witnesses, and spokespersons of the College. The question he has chosen bears the title "What came to pass?" Okay, so tell us, share with us: What came to pass?

J-LN:[3] At the time of the founding of the College, the primary motivation, it seems to me, and I believe it was the same for the founders, was to open up a place of expression for high school [*lycée*] teachers who wanted to do a certain kind of research and who did not have access to a university environment.

This was in response to a considerable mutation within philosophy, particularly in France, that had started about twenty years before the creation of the College. The students who had become teachers in the 1960s and 1970s had taken part in this mutation through their studies, which were themselves influenced in part by the innovative and invigorating ideas of the times. I know this from experience: my students during these years were working in the climate of the thinking of Derrida, Deleuze, Althusser, Lacan, and so on. As a result, teaching in high school was itself changing, not so much in the programs of study themselves, but very noticeably—just to stick to the most institutional signs—in the textbooks or in the choice and wording of the topics for the Baccalaureate exam.

In the beginning of the College, I experienced a certain disappointment at seeing the space of the College taken over by university professors, whose work, I recognized, was part of the general philosophical innovation or recasting of the times, though I understood less well why they sought out the space of the College, which was in some sense superfluous for them. That being said, I recognize that the exceptionally favorable conditions unique to Strasbourg allowed Lacoue-Labarthe and myself not to be in need of another place of teaching and expression.

Nevertheless, it seemed to me then and still seems to me today that the central mission of the College is to provide access for high school teachers to its seminars and programs. At the same time, motivated by GREPH, which was founded by Derrida and others, the idea of a more comprehensive reform in the teaching of philosophy in high school began to take shape, including its extension to before the final year, which of course implied the invention of new curricula and procedures.

The system of "course release,"[4] which was created in this spirit, has for a long time now facilitated the development of a climate in which a new articulation of philosophy in the university and in secondary schools might be carried out, as well as a new articulation of the school itself and of the relationship between philosophy and the school's democratic ends. Twenty years later, I continue to think that the College, through and in spite of its own difficulties, at once external and internal, will have, fortunately, contributed to supporting the needs of young philosophers and of philosophy as a living enterprise.

But it is impossible not to make a double observation. On the one hand, philosophical life in the university has continued to regain its safest and most safeguarded territories—the history of philosophy, the disciplines of argumentation and formal analysis—and, on the other hand, high school teaching proves itself to be every day less capable of truly integrating a philosophy whose practice, at least in the present conditions, is too closely tied to a classical culture from which students are today disconnected. At the level of language or of references, at the level of the mastery of discourses or of the perception of the evolution of Western thought, the gap has become enormous between the requirements of teaching as it is currently defined and the actual state of today's student population. (To put it rather bluntly, reading each year a certain number of Baccalaureate exams convinces me of the sterility and hypocrisy—at least when measured against the standard of the exam—of a teaching that seems, globally speaking, more in a mode of survival or self-defense than in one of growth and invention. This is but one aspect, perhaps the most symptomatic, of an ever-growing problem within teaching in general.)

The situation is thus, in a sense, reversed: the lines of communication between the university and the high school, between research and teaching, between philosophy and actual democracy are, as it were, all down, in trouble if not regressing. Instead of the College thus being, it seems to me, the interface it once was, I fear that it might now be stuck between orders, systems, or worlds that barely communicate. Where we wanted a bridge, we find an island. Where we hoped for a passage, we find a refuge. Of course, I am not blaming the College itself, nor any particular institution, not even the various governments in the intervening years. To be sure, a detailed analysis of the situation would find no shortage of legitimate critiques. But details should initially be of little concern, because it's a question of the whole: globally speaking, philosophy has come to stand at a growing distance from teaching—and by teaching I mean something other than its own internal reproduction, a democratic teaching not only in the sense of being "offered to everyone" but in the sense of "initiating, opening up, making democracy itself possible." This is in fact to say that philosophy has undergone a dehiscence, that it is dissident with regard to itself, that is, with regard to this closed construction of what might rightly be called, and not necessarily in a pejorative sense, the system of theoretical and symbolic references of the classical bourgeoisie. That's why it is not really possible, and it would in any case be insufficient, to engage in retrospective accusations: the phenomenon is of the order of culture—or of civilization—itself.

This dehiscence and this dissidence, to which the College has had to bear witness so as to have an effect in the two areas of teaching (university and high school) and so as to encourage interactions between these two orders, were not able to transform (to reform? to be themselves reformed by? these are open questions) the actual state of affairs, which is becoming more and more dire and which contributes in a paradoxical way to a greater and greater isolation of the College both from the university (even though, and this has been unexpected, reference to the College has become a positive credential on university résumés) and from high schools (where very young teachers often have none of the expectations for research and forums of expression as their older colleagues).

I have spoken only of the relationship of the College to the two orders of teaching: this is intentional, as I explained at the beginning. I am well aware of the College's important, indeed indispensable contribution to philosophical work in the public arena. I also congratulate it for its many seminars as well as its day-long events, its conferences, and its radio programs. They offer a program of very high quality, a space open to endless innovation. But let me simply note that this space tends to create a specific and original place rather than an organ of communication, transfer, or contagion.

There is, of course, nothing worrisome about a project being transformed as it evolves, develops, becomes more concrete. This is the normal fate of any living project. But such evolution will have in this case revealed, for philosophy in high school and in the university, a situation that is evolving in the sense of an involution and that is tending in the direction of a crisis that could be very serious—unless, and this is what seems most likely, we are already beyond the crisis and are now seeing the slow and irreversible mutation of the very idea of "philosophy in the democratic school." It is to this situation that the College, on this anniversary, which the College is right to want to celebrate and which I hope portends many more, might consider devoting particular attention.

One final word: it is not at all certain that philosophy as such should be part of teaching. After all, there have been entire epochs during which philosophy was being practiced apart from the university as well as from secondary schools. But it so happens that democracy imposes a very special definition of what is deemed necessary in teaching: it is no longer a question of simply mastering certain forms of knowledge necessary for work and, if need be, for leisure. At stake is a knowledge that is indispensable to the very exercise of democracy itself, to its being and its action. This knowledge can be called *philosophy* or something else; it is quite clearly implicated in more than one discipline and, in the end, in all of them, but what is essential is that it exists and exists with this in view.

JD: I think that you were, of course, right to recall that long before the official founding of the College a philosophical mutation had taken place in the 1960s (1968 through 1970) and that, without mentioning certain quasi-institutions—GREPH, the Estates General of Philosophy—it must be noted that between 1968 and the left's coming to power there had been in the so-called field of philosophy a—to put it very bluntly—public regression, accompanied by a whole series of publications that found echoes in the most widely read newspapers and magazines of the times and that went under the name, for example, of *la nouvelle philosophie, les nouveaux philosophes* ("the new philosophy"; "the new philosophers"). During the years 1974–75 to 1980, the *nouveaux philosophes* were those who at once denied and obscured, each time in a different way, what had happened in the 1960s and 1970s, which remains for us a major reference. There was even, during the Estates General of Philosophy, in the auditorium where it was taking place, a skirmish that almost came to blows—there are still photographs of this—between certain representatives of this *nouvelle philosophie* (I won't name any names) and some of us.

There was thus a conjunction between the refusal of this regression, whose defects we all saw—lack of philosophical rigor, ideologization, a thirst for media attention—and the left's coming to power. At the Estates General, we called—just as GREPH had done—for extending the teaching of philosophy into secondary schools. And we asked François Mitterrand to include in his program the development of the teaching of philosophy. We had hoped—and we were disappointed—that he would keep his word. But in any case, even if he failed to do so, at the time of the Haby Reform the prevailing winds were nonetheless in support of philosophy's fight, although many among you may not know that.[5] In fact, I don't really know who is here exactly. I wanted earlier to pose a school-inspector type of question by asking François Noudelmann just how many people there are in the College Assembly and about how many are here today, and what is the average age.

I still recall—to recount an anecdote—my disappointment at something that occurred during the first year of the College. I was director at the time, and I had succeeded in inviting, in the name of internationalization, a Japanese philosopher who was the first foreigner to speak here, in this very auditorium. I was very proud of this initiative. Well, there was hardly a single member of the College present on that occasion. And this pattern continued for a long time, as far as I know. I don't know how many members of the College have read the *Rapport bleu*, how many are interested in the genealogy of the College. I would be very interested to know to what degree they are interested in such things, whether they know where the College comes from, and I wonder whether there shouldn't be a sort of genealogical initiation whereby members are cloistered for a couple of weeks to study the origins of the College.

J-LN: Yes, but you see, Jacques, I said earlier that "the Republic was indeed hovering over the cradle of the College." You just said so. It was Chevènement.[6] I had forgotten about this. I think it's very significant. I wonder in fact if it makes sense to say that the only difference between a government of the left—and thus, as it would happen, a republican minister—and governments of the right is that the governments of the left, to the extent that they were still republican or, let's say, in a spirit that is related to this, could expect a College of Philosophy to provide something like a philosophy—I'm not sure what to call it—not a philosophy of the state or of the government, that would be too crude, but something that would nevertheless come to cut a good figure. For it also has to be said that official philosophy, as it was represented by the curriculum of the *terminale*, that is, of the last year of high school, and by the organization of higher education that led to this official philosophy, had come to cut a pretty sorry figure and had to be abandoned. I think there might have been this expectation, followed by disappointment at what actually happened in the College, and this was followed by the indifference you've just mentioned.

JD: And we also know that, in the tradition you are recalling, the oldest French tradition, each time it became clear, for one reason or another, that a certain number of things could not be done in the university, a parallel institution was created right next to the university in an attempt to remedy some of its shortcomings. That was obviously the case of the Collège de France, which initially did not include philosophy but was devoted to classical languages. It was also the case of the Écoles Pratiques des Hautes Études,[7] where certain subjects that couldn't be taught at the university could be taught in this parasitical, marginal, even secondary institution, which was created in opposition to or in the margins of the university. In other words, a certain weakness in the university in France has each time led to a deficiency, which has then led to the birth of an institution that, despite everything, despite being the initiative of the powers that be, remained different and marginal.

J-LN: Jacques, if you will allow me, I would like to say something that I forgot to say earlier. Speaking of moments of enlightenment, it is remarkable that the Enlightenment is a time when the university was almost totally worthless, not only from the point of view of philosophy—okay, despite Wolff—but from the point of view of all areas of knowledge. Modern science, all modern fields of inquiry, were invented outside the university. It's not a question of stigmatizing the university, but I think that's the way it is in the university: there are empty periods and periods of solidification. And what's rather remarkable is that this was in fact the case of the Enlightenment.

JD: Obviously—we were speaking of democracy earlier—the model that we set for ourselves in the concept of the College, in its functioning, its representativeness, its structures, and its modes of work, was an ideal model of democracy. There was no position that could be taken for granted, nothing that was not subject to election or reelection; there was an unconditional independence with regard to exterior powers. Now, to be realistic, this independence was never unconditional, but unconditionality was inscribed or prescribed, in some sense, in the first projects of the College.

Like you, I would use the [French] word *invention* in its double sense. There is, first of all, the *invention* that discovers what was already there, what was hidden there, and that, in some sense, takes note of what is possible; the *invention* of the body and the fact that it discovers—this is an act; it's an event, but the event consists in revealing or unveiling something that was already there. And then there is the *invention* that consists in producing, sometimes technically, an object that did not previously exist. Well, it was this double concept of *invention* that guided us, since it was a question of taking note of everything in what had happened and in what was happening that was, to our eyes, most powerful and most interesting, not only in philosophy but between philosophy and the sciences and the arts, and then also, all the while actively taking note of this, producing new objects, and not only theoretically but practically—performative objects, we might say. From the beginning, it was specified in the *Rapport bleu* that the College would help give rise not only to theoretical works of teaching and research but to artistic acts, to musical or visual productions, and we were very attached to this double vocation, to the institution itself being a technical invention. There is no institution in the world, as far as I know, whose model is really identical to that of the College. I'm talking here about the model.

It was thus a matter of inventing and reinventing, with all the risks this involved. One of the rules was that, without ever going to war against the university—for we insisted on this a great deal, we were not about to enter into open conflict with the university, indeed, we looked to create alliances with universities, and some of these worked better than others—we would privilege the objects, themes, and problems that were not legitimized by the university or similar institutions. And that too was part of the imperative for invention that we set for ourselves.

So, what happened philosophically in the course or these twenty years? Even though I have, like everyone here, a good deal of information about what happened, many impressions and readings of what happened or did not happen, or happened only to a small extent, I am incapable of saying what happened in philosophy over these twenty years. I am not saying that nothing happened, but I would be unable to give it a name, to provide a concept for it.

J-LN: But Jacques, it seems to me that . . .

JD: What I am saying is not negative. It's just that I myself would be unable to formalize it.

J-LN: Yes, but I might be so bold as to try to formalize things just a bit—really just a bit, even crudely—based on what I said earlier. I think that what happened was the end of all *Weltbilder*. What has been called, in a more Nietzschean-Heideggerian vocabulary—though also a little bit

Derridean—the *end of metaphysics*. Because this *end of metaphysics*, which would take us back to the 1920s, was the common observation of people like Heidegger, Wittgenstein, and Freud. If I name those three, it's because it's a quasi-quotation of Bouveresse, who says somewhere that it is those three who had to bear witness to something like the *end of metaphysics*, or what Heidegger called the *end of philosophy*, which people then stubbornly refused to understand in the sense that he meant it.

And it might be said that this trio—which, if I am not mistaken, Bouveresse evokes, the trio of Heidegger, Wittgenstein, and Freud— already indicates something about the different directions one might take from that point on. To put it very baldly, there is the *end of metaphysics* as it is understood by the likes of Gérard Lebrun, a great friend who has left us—and I am not mentioning him in order to criticize him. By entitling his book *Kant and the End of Metaphysics*, he was suggesting that "the speculative is over and done with," and a great deal of what is happening in the university today seems to me to be guided by this thought. On the other hand, there is the very large Heideggerian filiation, which must be extended all the way to Deleuze, without any paradox, I believe, where the *end of metaphysics* means the *invention*, the *reinvention of metaphysics*. That's a large part of what happened.

JD: These past twenty years?

J-LN: Yes, I would say so. But it had been played out before that. In the last twenty years, I would say that it's not this that got played out. What got played out is the increasing competitiveness and the institutional, political, and social rigidification of this division. And there remains the third, Freud, whose place would be much more difficult to determine. But Freud, and those who follow him, are now facing a problem of institutionalization, and this is certainly no accident: it's the history of the amendment, the law. That's not saying very much, but it is nonetheless very striking that, if we hold onto this idea that there were these two lineages or two genealogies, it so happens that the university— and, here again, what goes along with it, secondary education—now follows one of these directions.

JD: I wouldn't say that nothing happened philosophically over these twenty years, that there haven't been great and important books, but these rarely came from the university properly speaking. I'm saying that this did not take the form of a configuration that would be, I dare not say, "dominant," but at least visible as such. And I would compare this—which I hold to be a fact—to what happened in the College, where, on the one hand, I was among those who regretted that there was no seminar of the College itself, that is, one that would have brought together the members of the College without any public, as it were, in order to carry out among themselves a work in common. As a result, there was a dispersion, for all sorts of reasons, and sometimes for good reasons—because it wasn't technically possible, or because people didn't have the time—and so the works of the College remained, and this is not necessarily a shortcoming, dispersed, so to speak, in their philosophical trajectory. There was not, during these twenty years—and this is to be at once celebrated and somewhat regretted—a philosophical spirit [*esprit*] of the College. I am not saying a doctrine or a school of the College, but there was not even any sort of original philosophical configuration that could be recognized, that would be recognizable from the outside. There have been, undeniably, many very rich works, diverse works, but nothing that would gather these works in a configuration that would bear the mark, the brand, of the College. I am not sure if I am going too far here or if I am mistaken.

And this is not unrelated to the fact that outside, in the space outside the College, in the public philosophical space, there were no fronts either, so to speak. There are no fronts. And that's a big difference because there used to be fronts. Today, there are no fronts. Hence there might be very important, very powerful works, but the structure of the *Kampfplatz*, of the battlefield, has changed. There is no longer any battlefield. There are all kinds of insidious skirmishes that go by way of certain presses or publishers whom the participants frequent, but there is no great philosophical battlefield with fronts. And I think that between this dispersion of the works of the College and the lack of unification, of a battlefield, of a front, of philosophical confrontations, there is a certain relationship. We know that now.

J-LN: But now I would say that there is . . . I would first like to know whether you regret this state of affairs, because sometimes one gets the impression that you are some kind of Prussian General . . .

JD: No, no.

J-LN: "Ready the troops for battle!"

JD: No, I'm just taking note. We said in fact from the outset that we didn't want this.

J-LN: Yes, right. So it's a good thing it's not like that.

JD: No, what I am saying is totally contradictory, I am well aware. I am at once happy about this and I regret it. It's true. And then I just do my work. You know—if I may share something personal here—I have loved the College a great deal, having been among those who dreamt of it and founded it. But I found rather quickly that I could not remain in the College. First of all, the administrative responsibilities of director are too onerous. And then, in general, I am not enough of a communitarian to bear being part of a clan. So I quickly withdrew, all the while retaining my sympathies, my solidarity, and my friendship for the College and for many of its members. But as a space it did not suit me.

J-LN: Yes, but that being said, I who am communitarian—and much too much for your taste—have observed that through the College in part, not only but nevertheless to a great deal through the College over these last twenty years, no front has formed, this is true, but solidarities have been established—a bit like a network—between very different kinds of people, and so one can find in these solidarities people who wouldn't have been there at the beginning of the College: people like those I just mentioned, the Wittgensteinian branch, which is itself very complex, even if rather small, and which I would not want to reduce to a very false idea of what comes from Wittgenstein. And so, speaking for myself, I have the feeling that at this time in France and in the world there are also strong solidarities, which we could mark with colored thumb tacks on a philosophical world map. That exists, you know.

FRANÇOIS NOUDELMANN: To come back for a moment to the definition of the College, something was quite noticeable in your exchange: Jacques Derrida brings together a certain voluntarism and a symptom of today's intellectual and philosophical life. And Jean-Luc Nancy also sketched out a sort of opposition, it seems to me, between, on the one hand, the Republic—and this was an important moment, there was a sort of Republican will to create the College, without necessarily defining a Republican philosophy—and, on the other hand, this whole social need. This is a well-known opposition between society and the state. You also evoked, Jean-Luc Nancy, globalization, the need for philosophies to understand what is happening. The College is made up of this voluntarism of individuals or of the state and then also of this need that leads it to transform itself.

JD: I think that one homage that must be paid to the College of today or of yesterday—not necessarily the College of before yesterday but of yesterday and of today—is that it excluded nothing, in sum. Or rather, it excluded things of poor quality, while opening itself up on as many sides as possible. And that is a very good thing; it is one of its most positive aspects—the College's hospitality. It is one of the most remarkable places of hospitality there is. I say this in all sincerity.

NATALIA AVTONOMOVA: I am not here to thank anyone in particular, but I will allow myself nevertheless to throw a bit of external light on what has been discussed here, which is truly fascinating. Jacques spoke of the *Rapport bleu*; I was reading this *Rapport bleu* on the plane and kept saying to myself: "It's truly incredible, there is always in France this spirit to create structures that exist nowhere else, precisely like the International College of Philosophy, or the Collège de France, or the École des Hautes Études." And now, as you are discussing things that are extremely important—about philosophy, different aspects of philosophy, research and teaching, teaching in high schools or universities—I cannot help but feel the enormous difference between the environment in which I usually find myself in my country, where the question of teaching philosophy in high school would have been, I would say, a blessing for people. One can only hope for this; it does not exist.

And so when Jean-Luc says there are bad aspects and good aspects, that there are all kinds of problems with this arrangement, one is nevertheless discussing, defending the possibility of teaching philosophy, and there are other countries where this can be seen, and in my view this has enormous repercussions on the shaping of the mindset of their citizens. I also see this in certain aspects of the history of my country, Russia, where a lack of conceptualizing philosophy also has repercussions today; and the difficulties of developing this type of philosophy were palpable during the Soviet and pre-Soviet eras and are still being felt today, and this is regrettable. But really, there are all kinds of ways of doing this, in order finally to be able to speak conceptually with other philosophies, and not just to hide behind religious or other ways of thinking.

I was thus particularly interested in Jean-Luc Nancy's comments when he spoke of the lack of common ground that sometimes exists between the conceptual side and the intuitive side in contemporary philosophy, as it is developing here in France. It's a real problem, this disparity between different aspects of philosophy, as he put it, between formalisms and historicisms. It's a little vague. It is all the more important where I come from, having discussions with people who have their own problems, which are also mine, since I am here as a program director of the College. When I said in my initial remarks that the title of my program is not translatable, it means that there are all sorts of conflicts in the community that speaks of philosophy in the world. We cannot just measure ourselves against the standards of Western contemporary thought. This has to be put in other terms. We have to acknowledge that there are always inter-influences, inter-relations.

There are thus resistances, difficulties, always all sorts of political, economic, financial considerations, intellectual as well. But I said to myself that, nevertheless, it is good to celebrate this absolutely incredible and unique thing that is the College and to see the productivity of its contradictions.

MICHEL DEGUY: I'm reminded all of a sudden of the sometimes heated discussions with Régis Debray. In the end, one could sum up the criticism in this way: "If Saint Paul had acted like us (like Debray), there would be no Christianity." In other words, from a methodological point of view, he found the College to be too fragile, too, so to speak, feeble-minded. In other words, it's a question of the right measure of non-fragility and fragility in order to be able to subsist—something of that sort.

MARIE-CHRISTINE LALA: I would like to recall, since it is important to know where we are all coming from when we speak, that when I was a high school teacher in the north I was able to teach at the College a seminar on Georges Bataille; this was in 1986, 1987, and 1988. For the last ten years I have been teaching in the university—I am thus a university professor—and I have once again the opportunity to speak about Georges Bataille in this same forum. And I must say that given the nature of Bataille's work in relation to thought, this is the only place where I can speak freely of Bataille. I thus wanted to add a bit to the discussion insofar as you raised the issue of the status of this institution. It seems to me that we've only just touched upon some very important topics, and I was bit worried at a certain point when you, Jean-Luc Nancy, spoke, because I had the impression that we were holding an Estates General of Philosophy and that the state of affairs was rather depressing. And it is true that right now in the university one can say that what's going on is bad, yes, but we can ask whether we have to accept it, whether it is necessary or not. And speaking for myself, I am in the middle of this debate and I am suffering from it, because it's very difficult. And I tell myself that, perhaps, we have here, not a key to, exactly, but an idea of how to position ourselves for the future. And you said—and I don't agree with this—that the College could be considered an institution in the position of institutionalization. I am very bothered by this notion, because when one says *position* one can also very quickly say "in the process of institutionalization," and I don't think that that is either desirable or in the character of the College, since it would then no longer be the College. As for me, I would rather speak of a trans-institutional institution. And you said at a certain moment that it is indeed an institution that allowed passage between spaces—and I rather agree with that. I think that one must be very careful when one raises this problem of the institution of the College, because one might wish simply to remain at that level. At the same time, we all know very well that it is an institution that is neither like the Collège de France nor like the École des Hautes Études en Sciences Sociales; it's a place where one can talk about things one cannot talk about elsewhere, and in particular, I would say, about the work of thought itself, something that is extremely difficult to pursue. There you go. This is a question that perhaps ties in with the exchange you've had. Jacques Derrida, thank you very much for the way you have posed the question. You've spoken of those undocumented people [*sans papiers*] who are academics and yet are not recognized. I think it's the problem of a certain relationship to the Law that is being posed here. It's a question addressed to the two of you, I think, a question of the naming of what is, for me, this trans-institutional institution.

JD: That's not quite what I said. As for what is happening in the university, I would like to say—because I said at one point that I was not here to make value judgments, since all this is, clearly, very complicated—that, like you, I too taught courses on Bataille around 1975, but that was many years after leaving the university. Let's take this as a symbol, a symptom—and for many reasons. But certainly also because the university did not lend itself to it, nor did its students. The university today is undergoing important transformations in terms of its audience. And this is happening—it has to be said—because the politics of the democratization of the university in France has been, I think, very poor, botched, misplaced, and has in fact imperiled the university in France much earlier than in other countries, such as Germany, England, or even Italy. There are questions that are specific to each country. But there is also for the university a general question, which is obviously, it seems to me, that of the necessity of completely redefining today what a university is.

M-CL: If I may be allowed to rephrase things just a bit, because when I spoke of "the only place that allowed me to speak of Bataille in complete freedom," I also meant to say that there are in the university departments defined by disciplines. And that's good. One thus cannot speak about Bataille in the same way in a department of philosophy as in a department of literature, given these imperatives. And I believe that when I said "the only place" this was not restrictive with regard to the university: that is, there are certain limits that are imposed by university teaching and that the College allows one to go beyond, because of these passages, these interfaces that are its vocation. It's in this, in fact, that it's not to be opposed to the university.

JD: Yes, but there are in foreign universities departments that are founded upon inter- or trans-disciplinarity.

M-CL: Yes . . . or else this trans-disciplinarity is rejected, as was the case with our universities, because there is also this dimension in the French university at its origin.

HÉLÈNE CIXOUS: Just a few words, because I would feel guilty if I didn't say them. It's a sort of testimony as well as a reflection. I would like to say that the mutation we have been talking about, what has changed over the last twenty years—more than twenty years—has to be given the name of Jacques Derrida, that is, what has truly transformed the space or the field of philosophy in an inescapable, non-measurable, and totally decisive way is the thought of Jacques Derrida. I don't have any problems putting it like this; I prefer to affirm it. And I would also like to say that the metaphor of the battlefield is not only a metaphor. I cannot imagine not being permanently embattled. Everything that would not be a battle—I have no hesitation here, not even Jacques's hesitation—everything that is not embattled, in my opinion, does not produce, does not make anything, does not create. We are embattled and the College is a curious theater of operations for a certain battle that remains fairly restrained, that is not violent, but still . . .

And this is where the question of testimony comes in. I hesitated, in fact, to say this, but I have to do so, if only because we were mentioned earlier by Jacques, and because François Noudelmann was following the tradition of welcoming that you earlier called "hospitality." And so I would like to return to this word *welcoming*: there is a politics of welcoming in the College, not just at a strictly interdisciplinary, international level, but for refugees. I here represent these refugees. It is very important to say this, because I know that no one is aware of this. But one should know that the program I created in 1974 under the title Doctorate in Women's Studies, in order to hide behind an institutional shield, was never legitimated. Still today, we are illegitimate. If there had not been the College of Philosophy to give us shelter, I would have long ago fled the battlefield, and, in any case, we would have been wiped out.

You should know—and I'm now coming back to the question of the university—that the university, my university, which I myself founded, namely Paris VIII, has always been our enemy, always, right up to today, and today more than ever, and if we had not had the possibility of a fallback position, of a strategic retreat, some safe haven—and that is why I really think in terms of refuge—I would not have been able to continue to pursue the kind of philosophico-literary teaching that has never been accepted, that will always be fought. I thus want to say thank you—I'm not sure exactly to whom; to individuals. And I wish to underscore this aspect of the individual. I recall having seen again Mr. Lesgards to beg him to help us—and he did. I've seen more than one president or director of the College. And the last—whom I did not have to solicit because he came to me—was precisely François, who has my endless gratitude. All this time we have been saying here *the* [le] College. But it's nevertheless a complicated collective. *The* College is also sometimes *an* individual; it's a grouping whose users, I have to say, don't even know its composition most of the time. One might say that this is not good, but I say it's very good. It's very good that *the* College be a sort of title that, in truth, has a certain suppleness, even a laxity, which benefits many, including us. And I don't dare describe to you what can go on in universities for those who are not in them, but you should know that in the university what gets formed in an insidious way are communitarist communities of colleges, what are called colleagues, but who are also enemies. It must be said that the College has never produced or let be produced by definition, by structure, anything like this communitarism of the university, which is absolutely deadly and self-perpetuating—and self-perpetuating because of its way of recruiting. For, as you know, universities self-recruit. It is thus always according to the same model that such repressive structures get reproduced ad infinitum.

I must say that *the* College, with all its faults and shortcomings, even its ongoing naïveté, is nonetheless an extremely precious place. And it owes this once again to its founding. I insist on speaking of the origin. The origin is decisive. The few people who founded it at the outset were, for the most part, well aware that even Paris VIII, the most experimental of universities, was crippled and nasty, and so they sought to put up a tent for nomads. I would adopt quite gladly the term *passer*: this is a place of passers and of passages. And then there are passers, like me, for example, in the university, who need passers—there can thus be passers for the passers, even if one can ask the question of the witness for the witness. So there you go. Now don't go and denounce me, now that I've told you that we have been clandestine in the College. That would be a real problem.

ALAIN DAVID: I too am a refugee, if you will, since I am one of those program directors who come out of secondary education and to whom the College offered a place, the possibility of things that have been for me quite wonderful. And I don't know how to say and express my gratitude sufficiently. But at the same time, I think that if there were only that, it would not be enough, or at least it would be absolutely excessive to think that the College was created for my sole benefit or for the benefit of a certain number of other teachers from secondary schools like myself, or for others who seek refuge and who, for a time, are given a place of expression. I think there is something else. In fact, the temptation would be to think or to believe, at least as concerns secondary schools, that the College offers a kind of jump seat, in view of the university, for doing a dissertation or, beyond the College, finding a position within the university.

I want to say instead that the presence within the College of program directors coming from secondary schools has a completely different meaning. And I can attest to the fact that the program directors play an extremely active role inside the College, perhaps more active or at any rate just as active as the program directors coming from the university. But this is just a symptom. I think that, at bottom, secondary schools represent first and foremost, in relation to the university, a secret finality or end, and the university is in the end largely motivated, carried along by what is happening downstream, in secondary education. The university does not always know this, and secondary education does not always know it either. One sometimes has the impression that secondary education has ended up believing that it is in some sense the ante chamber of the university, a university conceived as a place of knowledge with certain standards of excellence. But what is happening within secondary schools and what is coming out of them is, I believe, something else altogether. I don't have the time or the possibility to say much more about this here, but I might put it in just a few words by evoking Kant's expression regarding our "common rational knowledge of morality." Something like that comes out of secondary schools. And I believe that the College is a place that is capable, or that might be capable, of taking this up and of addressing it to the university, by representing in relationship to the university this place where something completely different in philosophy is able to be expressed. It is this address, I believe, that we must take into consideration and that we must privilege in relation to the university, in order to address ourselves to the university, not in the sense of a critique or in the sense of a denigration of the university, but in order to let pass through this other expression, the expression of a philosophy inventing itself from out of philosophy as a living enterprise, as Jean-Luc Nancy said earlier.

CHAPTER FOUR

Responsibility—Of the Sense to Come
(2002)

FRANCIS GUIBAL: I won't be so foolish as to try to introduce Jacques Derrida here. I know that there are many among us who are grateful for everything he has brought to thinking, brought into in our space of language and of writing, and we are happy to see the continuation of exchanges with Jean-Luc Nancy that are neither simply self-serving nor self-satisfied but that, it seems to me, intersect and, so to speak, fecundate one another. I think that we are now going to see how this will continue. Let me thus give Jacques Derrida the floor right away and thank him again.[1]

JD: *Future, mother, father, fecundity*: these words have been nagging us since earlier today. I will not flee from them. Thank you, Francis Guibal and Jean-Clet Martin, for having taken this very felicitous initiative. I think I can speak on behalf of everyone here—since this is the last session—and declare to you our immense gratitude. We were all looking forward to this event.

Just one question: Is one responsible for what happens [*arrive*]?

I could stop right there . . .

Another way of putting the same question would be: Isn't a decision always unjustifiable? Can one be or not be responsible for an event? And for a singularity, for the singularity of an event?

These uncertainties will remain suspended, as if in exergue.

You are probably very tired. Tiredness or fatigue might be a theme to reawaken. It was fashionable before and after the war. It was a topos for existential or existentialist philosophy. It was a question at that time of an ontological fatigue, if not a *fatigue of* ontology. A few decades ago, it was discussed quite a bit around Levinas and Bataille, to whom we should also add Blanchot and others. You are probably tired by all this talk, and not only because of the time that passes, but perhaps also because of the affect produced by what Jean-Luc Nancy yesterday called a sort of general equivalency. Our situation of thought, our "conjuncture," no doubt remains to be defined or thought. Without consensus, we are in fact struggling in a sort of dangerously common place. In the same place, the call to the event, to singularity—that is today no doubt the most commonly shared thing in the world, perhaps a bit too much so.

So, how are we to begin or begin again this evening without giving in to all these sorts of fatigue? Many among us here have written extensively on the themes announced and treated since yesterday. And written about them usually better than when we speak about them. At least I hope that is my case. What we should do here, if something still needs to be done, right at this moment, is speak as if we were beginning to speak, as if we were going to make something happen or come, that is, produce an event while improvising. Improvisation was part of the contract between Francis Guibal, Jean-Clet Martin, Jean-Luc Nancy, and myself.

The words I have just used, "to make something happen," "to make an event come" will perhaps serve here as a matrix. I use the word *matrix* because we all know since yesterday that Jean-Luc Nancy is the mother of us all: he conceives, he gives birth, and this morning we found out that his concepts get or sleep around [*découchaient*]. Jean-Luc is a mother who begets [*accouche*] and gets around [*découche*]. I thus won't refrain from speaking of a matrix.

"To make happen": that may be the matrix of the questions I am about to ask him.

I will give myself two rules, two prescriptions, two laws. Rather than give them to myself in an autonomous fashion, I receive them heteronymously. This couple (autonomy and heteronomy) will be inscribed right on the matrix.

The first law is to stick as close as possible to the title, and thus to the words and themes assigned by the organizers, Francis Guibal and Jean-Clet Martin. Let me read them: "Responsibility—of/for the sense to come [*Responsabilité—du sens à venir*]," with a hyphen that induces all the necessary turbulence into the phrase.

Second, the other law—that of asking just a few questions of Jean-Luc Nancy, and of drawing all of these questions from my wonderment as a grateful reader. And only so as to give him a pretext for speaking more than he has been able to do since yesterday. To tell us more, for our pleasure. Just another word, then, before moving on to questions that will all come down, no doubt, to the question of *making and/or letting come, making and/or letting the singular event take place.*

We would then follow this question back to that of a possible or impossible responsibility regarding sense and ab-sense (the absence of sense).

These preliminary words would thus express my grateful wonderment. I have said this elsewhere, and I thus repeat it with a bit more specificity: my grateful wonderment for the extraordinary fact that Jean-Luc Nancy, as we all know, has the courage, dare I say the heart, to take on the heritage, and not only to *make do with* the tradition, with the greatest, the most venerable lineage, to *live with it*, but to face all the immense conceptual ghosts that some among us, me in any case, had believed or deemed to be as fatiguing as they are fatigued: *sense*, to begin with, and then *world*, and then *creation*, and then *community*, and then *freedom*—so many themes he has confronted head on, while others, including me, were fleeing, trying to justify or organize our flight.

Yesterday, I was both delighted and in full agreement when Catherine Malabou stated, for example, that the word *existence* does not have the status of a "fundamental" concept in my work. She is right. I could explain why, though I will not do so here and now. But then I said to myself: in the end, besides this word, beyond this word, this concept, let someone find a single word or concept that plays a "fundamental" role in my work. There is none. All you have to do is read. There is none and there never was any. And for good reason.

My wonderment stems from the fact that Jean-Luc, in a lucid way and without simply returning to the past, took charge, so as to treat in a deconstructive, post-deconstructive, manner, these great themes, these great concepts, these great problems, that have as names *sense, world, creation, freedom, community*, and so on. Since I am still referring to Catherine Malabou's presentation, there was for me yesterday a moment of great pleasure—a suspect pleasure, no doubt, but a pleasure that I at least admit to—when she was talking about honey, about a honey that one pours in such a way that the honey runs on top of the honey. As for the honey and the historical situation we are discussing, as well as the question of a possible difference between Jean-Luc and me, a difference that, as those who pay us the honor of reading us know, is less a difference in position or philosophical thesis than in our way or manner of doing things, a difference in body precisely, in flesh, in style, in gesture; my sense is that I find myself in front of this tradition, with all those words, like a fly that has understood the danger. This makes me think of what I saw in my childhood, in the sweltering houses of Algeria, where in the daily fight against flies we would hang strips of paper covered with honey, flypaper, on which flies would land and then be caught, glued fast. Well, before all these great philosophical concepts of the tradition that Jean-Luc revisits in an incomparable way, I have always had the reflex to flee, as if, upon first contact, indeed merely upon *naming* these concepts, I were going to find myself, like a fly, with my legs glued: captured, paralyzed, held hostage, trapped by a program.

That is the reason why I was objecting earlier; even the word *body* is something like that honey, if not the same as it. Even if for a time and for strategic reasons I accept such a word, soon I no longer want to have anything to do with it. The body is the opposite of mind or spirit, and I know that I will get caught in the old honey of this binary opposition, between Platonico-Cartesian dualism and the "flesh" of our contemporary neo-phenomenologists. As for Jean-Luc, he goes straight at it with his *Corpus.* There is here, then, a source of wonderment over our differences in approach, in the way we approach honey or temptations, philosophical sweets or nutrients.

Let me go back to my first question: Can one be responsible for an event? Is there any sense in talking about a responsibility for the event? With regard to the event? Is this concept of the event, which we all hold so dear—it belongs to the so called general equivalency—compatible with the demand for responsibility, of which we have had many examples since yesterday? We are all, and Jean-Luc more than most, *against* irresponsibility, and first of all against philosophical irresponsibility. Let me thus repeat: Is one, can one be, responsible for an event? For what happens?

Even though I gave a seminar on responsibility for more than ten years, I am going to try to articulate my question in, one might say, a fresh, disarmed, and completely preliminary way.

If being responsible, if to assume, as we say, a responsibility—which, in the tradition we come from, has always implied, and these are so many problematic concepts, decision, freedom, intentionality, the conscious

I—is to *respond*, to be responsible for, to respond to, to be responsible
and respond before, which requires both address and injunction, then
. . . The first of my four questions—and they all amount to the same in
the end—would be the following: Can one make oneself responsible
for something happening, something that, as such, as the happening of
something (what is commonly called the event), must be unforeseeable,
exceed the program, and naturally take by surprise not only the addressee
but also the subject to whom or by whom it is supposed to happen? Can
one make oneself responsible without neutralizing the eventness [*événemen-
tialité*] of the event? Isn't to be responsible for an event to neutralize
precisely its irruption as event? If I say: okay, I can be responsible for
this, I can sign this, that means that I can produce it, that I am capable
of producing it, that this event is within my power. It thus does not affect
me as an event that would be truly irruptive, unforeseeable, singular, and
so on. In other words, between the concept of responsibility and the
concept of event, is there not, let's say, a sort of aporia?

J-LN: Yes, I agree. But I'd first like to say something, a bit in the
margins of your question-response, by referring to what you said before
beginning and to all the work that has been done here since yesterday. I
would like to say that our singular situation, today, in philosophy, has to
do (I was already saying this yesterday) with our not being in the classical
Kampfplatz, and in principle we haven't been there since Kant. We are
instead in a place where the hidden slipper of a general equivalency
moves about,[2] but without there being any consensus (that's what you
were saying).

The relationship between this remark and your question would be
this: all the work done since yesterday, this discussion as just one
moment in the middle of all this work, the work of all those who have
spoken here in such insightful ways, who are always approaching the
most difficult things, the most worried or worrisome things, all this work
brings me back, once again, to the following question: Who or what is
asking us to do this? To what are we responding here?

If I said yesterday, with a certain animation, that philosophers take on
political responsibility in doing their philosophical work, it was perhaps
because, in the end, doing this work amounts to trying to respond. This
is probably not exactly the question you are asking. You are talking about
responding to a question or a demand (I will come back to this distinction) that we do not know, or not exactly, and do not know whence it

comes. To take up Werner Hamacher's words from this morning, for example, does it come from a future or indeed from the absence of future, or, to use Alex García-Düttmann's terms, are we responding to or facing up to something that presents itself and conceals itself as something that would be self-evident?[3]

Are we not always in the process of responding? This itself already forms a question, and it takes us back perhaps to wondering whether, by distancing ourselves from all our origins or points of departure [*provenances*], as was said in this morning's discussion between Werner Hamacher and you, by detaching ourselves from all our points of departure (all the while reattaching ourselves to them, putting them back into play but without any warranty), we are nonetheless not responding to something—a question, demand, call, address, or injunction—that still comes from our point of departure? And that is the case, even if it comes without coming, as you said . . .

I am coming back to your question. I ask myself [*je me demande*]— and I ask you right away in turn—if in what calls for a response ("calls for a response"—that itself is already an interesting formulation) we are dealing with a question or a demand [*demande*]. We have long known, thanks to you in particular, that when it comes to the question we—how shall I put it?—have a problem, we have a demand, we have a question about the question. In the past, you were able to relate this logic, which you claim today is the logic of a response that is both programmed and programmatic, to the logic of the question, the logic of the question-response, the question *ti esti* being the paradigm and the *Inbegriff* of the question and of questioning in general ("being" being already given as an element of the response). And yet there remains something in the question that exceeds the program of the question-response and that is precisely that which *calls for a response* and that calls for a response even in the "what is?" question. What calls in this way is not what programs the response.

Is this what we should call the demand? What does demand mean and of what is it a demand? When we say "demand" and "demand for" something, for example, it seems to me that one always thinks, inevitably, of the demand for love, but what does that have to do with, for example, the demand for sense (and this, of course, is more than an example)?

And then we would have to think, next to the demand, in it or perhaps outside it, the address. Because in order for me to have to respond to something, it has to be addressed to me . . . My first reaction, there-fore, would be this: to the extent that to respond must make something happen, then there must be not just a response to the question but also, in the question or through the question, a response to a demand and to an address. And the two (or perhaps even three) responses are different.

Let's assume that to respond to a question entails being entirely within the program and in the case of the *ti esti* it is to be there where being is immediately assigned . . .

JD: To respond in a fitting way . . .

J-LN: Yes, to respond in a fitting way. If I were to ask, for example, "What is a microphone?" and I were to respond, "A microphone is an instrument that, and so on." That is the point of departure and the bare minimum of the ontologies to which Heidegger claims to address deconstruction. To respond to a demand, however, might consist in satis-fying or not satisfying the demand. There is a model of non-satisfaction for both the question and the response, and this came to me earlier when listening to you speak—it's a model I don't think you've ever used, and neither have I: the model of the Zen story. The general pattern of Zen stories, where wisdom comes in the guise of a joke, is, for example, the disciple who asks "Who is Buddha?" and the master responds "Shitty stick." He doesn't even say, if I am to believe my Zen masters, "It is a shitty stick." Indeed, he does not say "it is," he says "shitty stick," which is a response that is at once incongruous, incoherent, and asyntactical, and thus disappointing in many regards . . . But in Zen stories the response is always made up of both surprise and disappointment. It obvi-ously has to do with Zen archery, that is to say, with the art of hitting the target without aiming for it, a sort of non-intentional and thus non-phenomenological paradigm that we have perhaps never produced in the Western world.

Let's assume, then, that the response to the demand is a real response when it disappoints the demand, and let's assume that, perhaps (but I will leave this aspect aside), this is always what is at stake in the demand insofar as it is always, in some way, a demand for love. Let's assume that. Now, I would say that we must also respond to the address and that I can respond only if you ask me the question, if you address it to me. At this point, I hesitate. I say to myself, "Can I disappoint you?" In fact, I should have begun by saying to you "shitty stick," I totally blew it! . . .

JD: You think you would have disappointed me?

J-LN: Perhaps not, in fact: which proves that one cannot take you out of your own program! And so there is no point in going any further . . . The event will not take place . . .

But it seems to me that if the address probably can and even must always miss its mark, if it is always *destinerrant*, as you say, then there can be this whole configuration—question-demand-address and response—only if the address has somewhere awakened the possibility of the response and thus if, behind the response, there is something that I would want to call *resonance*. It has to resonate. It has to resound; there has to be some resonance—I will not go as far as to say echo insofar as an echo simply repeats (though echoing could be a very good form of a disappointing response, and one could make up a Zen story—there's a good chance it already exists—where the disciple asks "Who is Buddha?" and the master answers "Who is Buddha?" That's probably a good model. And it might tell us a good deal about the echo, and perhaps about narcissism . . .).

What is there to say here about responsibility? I cannot be responsible, in the sense of a programmatic, calculated, and calculating appropriation, either for what I respond or for the effect it produces, but I am at least responsible for the capacity, for the condition of possibility, of the response that is found within the resonance. When a question is addressed to me, it proposes two things at once: it questions, but simply through its address it touches upon a capacity for resonance—or else it does not. For if I do not respond at all, it no longer quite fits the model of the Zen story; it is a sort of reduction to zero of the Zen story, which can function only if the non-response is a silence. And silence is not simply non-response: it is in some way resonance itself. There is a silence through which, or in which, I let the address of the other resonate. But if the silence is instead without resonance, like a muteness that can be attributed to a lack of willingness or a lack of understanding of the question or an incapacity, and so on, then there is no response at all.

But what, then, is this responsibility of resonance or as resonance? It is an immeasurable responsibility. And what I wonder is whether all responsibility does not in the end refer in some way to this immeasurable. Even the most calculating, fiduciary logic of insurances knows the immeasurable when it comes to responsibility. In the responsibility to be found in insurance—and there is someone in France, François Ewald, who knows this very well—what is being calculated, as we all know well, and this is part of the calculation, is a sample taken from a whole that is, in principle, not strictly speaking infinite but incommensurable. I think there is responsibility in that sense: always against the backdrop of the incommensurable.

JD: Let me try to pick up there. It is true that I was keeping this question of the calculable in reserve in order to follow up on it later. In general, in the traditional concept of responsibility, one presupposes that responsibility must be calculable. I must know what I am responsible for and there must be a measure of responsibility. And yet, of course, in the logic that you've just alluded to and to which I subscribe, responsibility is infinite; thus it is not determinable. And in the end, formally speaking, that is what I wanted to suggest.

But before coming back to this, I would like to make two remarks about what you just said, in passing, about Echo. It is very important. In Ovid, as you know, Echo is forbidden by the jealous goddess to do anything other than repeat the last words of Narcissus. But, in repeating the last words, or rather the last syllables, in order to obey and at the same time disobey the law, that is, in order to say something in her own name by playing with language, she manages to produce a totally unforeseeable event for Narcissus. And for the forbidding goddess. That indeed is the problematic of narcissism . . .

Let me make a second, completely anecdotal remark. It concerns what I wanted to recount yesterday when the question of "S is P," the question of the predicative statement, came up. I recall that once, a very long time ago, I was giving a lecture in front of or under the authority of a chief inspector of schools who was my former professor in *Khâgne*,[4] Étienne Borne. At one point I said: "Nothing can resist the 'What is?' question." In this way I was designating a catastrophe, the all too powerful authority of ontology. The omnipotence of this question, this "what is?" question, was for me the thing to question, indeed, to deconstruct. But he, as chief inspector of schools, applauded: "There you have it, he put it very well, nothing can resist the authority of the 'what is?' . . ."

I am going to try to pick up on what you said about the demand for love in order to move on to the second wave of questions. If I respond to a demand for love in a fitting manner, that is, without producing a surprise or a surplus, a gift that was not calculable or, we might say, already articulated in the demand, I am not responding. In other words, in order to respond to it, I must respond in another way, elsewhere, and in a surprising fashion, a bit off, if you will, in order for there to be an event. At that moment, no one can assume the calculable responsibility for what is taking place.

And this leads me to the second series of questions, in the same space. They concern the gift, debt, and duty. As was the case when I was speaking earlier of responsibility and the event, these are not at all critical questions or objections. I find myself, as you do, constantly caught between two languages, and very often, too often, it happens that I put a great deal of emphasis on the responsibility to be assumed and then, at the same time, on the event, knowing quite well that the two types of discourses are, in some way, in an antinomic relation. Hence debt, duty, injunction, and gift. I would risk the proposition—which I have advanced elsewhere in a more developed way—that what one does out of duty, in the most rigorous sense of the term, implies the acquittal of a debt. It is in this way that one becomes responsible; indeed, this is the very exercise of responsibility: one acts out of duty, one pays off a debt, one gets inscribed in an economy of the law. As a result, one is not producing any event and is not acting in an ethical manner. In other words, the ethical event, if there is any, must lead beyond duty and debt. And so we come up against this illogical or aporetic logic of the gift [*don*] and of giving up, of abandonment [*abandon*], which we have been discussing since yesterday, and that of the sense—or rather the non-sense—of responsibility. Elsewhere, and again in a much more developed way, I have tried to underscore that the gift, insofar as it exceeds economic exchange, must not have any sense. If I give in exchange, or if I am aware of the fact that what I am doing is a gift and that it has for me the phenomenological sense of the gift, then I am not giving. In other words, the gift—if there must be one and if it must be an event—must lose its sense of gift. It must exceed the intentional awareness of the gift, exceed sense, and it is on this condition that there will be gift, if there is any.

If this is the case, can one be responsible, can one say that one is responsible, for a gift, and thus that one is a giver, a donor, or, inversely, because this holds for the other side as well, that one is indebted for a gift received? And to relate this to what was said yesterday and today (I do not reduce abandonment or giving up [*abandon*] to the gift [*don*], though there is a somewhat necessary semantic link between the two), where there is gift or abandonment, must there not be an absence of the

will to abandon, whence the question of letting happen rather than making happen? And where there is and must be abandonment without the
will to abandon, gift without the will to give, if I *want* to give, if I give
because I want to give, as soon as I am aware that I am giving, the gift is
immediately destroyed. Thus, the gift must not have any apparent sense,
neither for the giver nor for the receiver. The abandonment must exceed
all will to abandon. Now, where the will is in abeyance, what gets suspended along with it is intentionality, freedom, and, as a result, the classical notion of responsibility. At that moment, when the gift happens, if
it happens, no one is there, no one must be there, to be responsible for
it, to sign, to say "I give" or "I receive." As a result, sense, in the strongest
sense of the term, in the phenomenological sense of the term, the very
sense of the gift, of abandonment, of duty, of responsibility, of intention,
of signature . . . must be put in abeyance.

This is an aporia. I can describe the gift in this way only by giving to
the gift a certain sense on the basis of which I then say that the gift must
have no sense. And it is with regard to this aporia that the question
of responsibility gets posed, that is, the question of the philosophical
responsibility you spoke of earlier.

On the one hand, I must give without responsibility, without assuming, without claiming to assume, sign, or lay claim to the gift, and this is
the case whether it be given or received. But, inversely, I am not giving,
giving anything at all, if I give absolutely without knowing that I am
giving or if the other receives without any kind of experience of the gift.
It will be said that nothing happens either. Nothing that we know or are
aware of or even experience. And why not?

If we are dealing here with an aporia of sense, of the gift and of the
event, we have to address the displacement of the question of responsibility: What is to be done philosophically, how is one to respond in a
philosophically responsible way *for*—and *before*—this ineluctable aporia
(and I do indeed hold it to be ineluctable)? How is one to address this
aporia in language and in life, in existence? How is one to address it
without abdicating? For it is not a question of abdicating responsibility;
it is a question of the moment when responsibility becomes the most
incalculable, infinite, and, as a result, indeterminable. I have to admit
that I always find ridiculous and even obscene statements that allow one
to say "I am responsible here," "I assume responsibility for this," or "I
am the one who decides." It is an obscene presumption, a claim to sovereignty that, moreover, does not hold up before the terrible and ineluctable aporia I have just recalled. Nevertheless, it is not a question, just

because it is obscene, of saying that one must abdicate all responsibility. Hence responsibility, if there is any, summons us with regard to this aporetic situation and, to follow this wave of questions all the way to the end, I will return to what I tried to note elsewhere, to ask you what you think about this notion that whenever one addresses someone, speaks to someone, gives to someone, responds to someone, this must always be done, first of all, in the form of what is traditionally called a performative. It is for that reason, in fact, let it be said in passing, that when someone asks "What is this?" it is not a question that calls for responsibility. If I respond "this is that," no responsibility is assigned to me, at least not of the kind we are talking about. Thus, in general, it is through a performative that I say to the other, at least implicitly, "I am talking to you," "I give to you," or "I love you" . . . Thus the performative, defined in this traditional but, to my mind, unimpeachable way—at least to a certain extent—is a discursive situation (though it can also be meta-discursive, non-discursive) in which the speaking subject, as we say, legit-imated through a certain number of conventions, says "I can" or implies "I can do this." I can open the session, I can say "yes" on my wedding day, I can this or that—and it's always "I" in fact—and responsibility, the assuming of responsibility, is always performative (I sign, I say that, I do this or that, and I assume my responsibility). But the event, if there is any, defined in a rigorous and exacting way, must exceed all power, including all performative power. We traditionally say that the performa-tive produces events—I do what I say, I open the session if I am presiding over it, I produce the event of which I speak. In general, we thus relate the possibility of the event that is produced to a performative initiative and thus to a performative responsibility. But to the extent that there is such a performative responsibility, the event in question is neutralized, immediately annulled. I am not saying that nothing then happens, but what happens is programmable, foreseeable, controlled, conditioned by conventions. It can thus be said, I would dare say, that an event worthy of its name is an event that derails all performativity. Or at least, it assigns a rigorous limit to performativity. And, as a result, to responsibility inso-far as it is linked to a performative power. Whence the question of non-power [*l'impouvoir*] that Werner Hamacher talked about this morning. Isn't that what we are talking about when we speak of the powerless Messiah? When it comes, when it happens, there must be powerlessness, vulnerability. The one to whom this is happening, the living one—

animal or human—must not have any mastery over it, whether performative or some other kind. And thus, in such a case, no one (no so-called
subject saying "I," no ipseity) must be able to assume responsibility, in
the traditional sense of the term, for what happens. Whence the aporia
in which we all find ourselves when we insist on the exigency of our
responsibilities, on the one hand, and, on the other, on the necessity of
taking into account the singular event, that is to say, the unforeseeable
event, irreducible to the concept, and so on, in a word, the event of the
other, the coming of the other, or as other: unable to be appropriated.

This aporia is also the aporia of sense. The event has no sense from
the point of view of anticipation, of a phenomenological or ontological
horizon. The event does not have, it must not have, sense. The aporia in
which we find ourselves is indeed an aporia concerning (I keep on referring to the title of our session) the "responsibility—for/of/in the sense to
come." If there is a responsibility, it is no longer that of this tradition, a
responsibility that implies intentionality, subjectivity, will, a conscious I,
freedom, autonomy, sense, and so on. It is a question of another responsibility and thus of a radical mutation in our experience of responsibility.

Now the difficulty, naturally, the historical, ethical, political, juridical
challenge we face, is that we must *negotiate* . . . I will want to ask you
whether you agree with me up to this point before moving on to my
next question: we must *negotiate*—and it was of a transaction of this
kind that I spoke earlier, strategically, in a given situation, between two
exigencies of responsibility: the traditional one, which we must exercise
all the time, and the other, which may seem, when compared with the
first, uncontrollable, incomprehensible, irreducible, unassimilable, but
which is no less imperative for those who are sensitive to the injunction
of thought. We must negotiate, every day, at every moment, between
these two logics, which are not both logics of the *same* [même] responsibility, but "logics" (without logic) of responsibility *itself* [même]. It is
thus a question of the same or of the itself [*du même*], of ipseity (*metipsis-
simus, meîsme*), and thus of the possible as power (see Benveniste, to
whom I will return in a moment).

The responsibility to be assumed is and must remain incalculable,
unpredictable, unforeseeable, non-programmable. Everyone, at every
moment—and it's here that there's responsibility—must invent, not only
for him or herself every day, but for him or herself each time anew, the
responsibility he or she must assume in any given situation by negotiat-
ing between two seemingly incompatible worlds of responsibility. Let me
stop there.

J-LN: I am not certain that I agree entirely with the word *negotiation* . . .

JD: Then *transaction*, if you prefer. In other words, we work it out . . .

J-LN: Okay, we work it out . . . but I was thinking about the literal meaning of *negotiation*. It is the negation of *otium*; the negotiant is the one who busies himself, who is in business.

JD: Yes, who works.

J-LN: Who works, yes, it has to do with work. And let me say in passing that it is always for me a source of wonder and puzzlement (on which I have not, precisely, worked very much . . .) that in our civilization business should have such an important, structuring, founding place and, at the same time, be the object of permanent denigration or subordination. In fact, when you say "we must negotiate," this is not very satisfying; we are stuck between a traditional responsibility and another one. But in my unapologetic idealism, I would like to try at least to think the exigency or necessity of this negotiation more profoundly than as a mere stopgap.

What I mean is this: why do you think responsibility in this way, and why do I, and no doubt many others, agree with you? That is, why this thought? Because this thought begins by being nothing less than an attempt to respond to a world of calculated and calculating responsibility, a world in which we are coming to assign a responsibility for responsibility, in an ever more precise manner, by means of calculations that are increasingly more exact and more difficult. To come back to the question of insurance, we know that there can be today enormous quantitative problems—for example, after September 11 and each time a great catastrophe occurs. That is, we are in a world where responsibility contributes to the ever growing dominance, to speak very simply and like a certain Heidegger, of calculation, of calculating reason, and so on, and it is in relation to this that you put forward the other exigency that you say we must address and with which we must negotiate.

What I would like to say is that this is more than a negotiation; it is the call for unlimited, non-calculating responsibility—assuming that this is indeed a call you are issuing; it is a necessary call because it responds to a demand, an at least silent demand, that comes from the world in which we are. And that is the reason why I had some reservations when you said that the incalculable, incommensurable responsibility is necessary "at least for those to whom thought matters," or something like that. I was afraid you were being a bit too dualistic, as if there were those who can think unlimited responsibility and then those who must practice responsibility . . .

JD: That was certainly not my intention.

J-LN: Then one should at least say that thought matters for everyone, whether they know it or not. There must not be any ambiguity on this score . . . This whole business, in fact, goes way back, perhaps all the way back to the beginnings of philosophy and to the idea that philosophers must govern. This is an idea that has perhaps always been misinterpreted, at least in part . . . In saying this, I am myself, of course, opening the door to the greatest possible misinterpretations.

This allows me to return to one of those "large concepts," as you say—that of *sense,* which Francis Guibal and Jean-Clet Martin decided to use in the title of this conference. I retain this word because, for me, sense, the sense of sense, is a call that comes always from within any community or any world; it is a call to resist installation, calculation, domination, and so on. It is, asymptotically, a call to model or regulate oneself upon the impossible, according to the incalculable. That is why—all the while admitting that there needs to be a process of negotiation—I would say that this negotiation must itself be in some way ordered or—what's the right word here?—regulated by that which gives no rules or regulations. That's a first element of response.

But in addition, to go deeper into your question, I would say this: it seems to me that you are suggesting that the gift be thought first of all as given up or abandoned. In order for the gift to be gift, it must really be abandoned. But then I could turn things around and ask whether the abandoned gift is not in fact calling forth, as a sort of echo, the abandonment that is given, whether the surprise and the disappointment of the response we discussed earlier were not perhaps the gift of abandonment. I am abandoning you . . . I am not responding to your demand with something that fulfills or satisfies it. The abandonment that is given is, in a certain way, the exposure to the impossible or the incommensurable that is itself given as an effect of the gift. When I give, I give or I expose the other to this gift as to something whose debt he or she will not be able to pay off and that thus, in some way, exceeds from the start the system of debt. But everything you say amounts also to saying that when gifts enter into an exchange of gifts—I offer you a tie, you offer me a tie, or you offer me a pipe or, on the contrary . . .

JD: What examples!

J-LN: Exactly, I stopped smoking a long time ago . . .

So, as you may have already guessed, I am coming back, in a rather circuitous way, to the heart of Christianity and of monotheism in general. For isn't it this absolute, infinite, unlimited responsibility, along with a debt that is also unlimited, that has taken on the figure of original sin?

That we may, and that we must, interpret the whole question of original sin and salvation in terms of a formidable economy is a given. At the same time, however, this formidable economy also represents an abandonment, and perhaps today we have reached the point where we must acknowledge, and whether this is with or without this point of origination is another question, that there is here a gift that is what it is—the gift of God, the creation of man—only insofar as it is abandonment, or the gift of an abandonment. There are some very great mystical traditions in the three monotheisms that move in that direction. To pick a recent, completely modern one, this is very present in Simone Weil, this idea that to create is to abandon what is created to its created condition. Man is abandoned. Let's leave aside what is called sin, or else let's assume that this sin is essentially made to be pardoned, or redeemed, or what have you. But this pardon or this redemption can be granted only by the one who, precisely, has given, the one who thus gives redemption as he gives sin, beyond all measure, according to something that cannot even be said in terms of justice, but that is called grace, grace as a sort of extremity that all justice ends up reaching, as Nietzsche writes somewhere . . . The gift of grace can come only after the gift of abandonment: two incommensurabilities.

Let me ask: Isn't there something that engages a beyond of all calculable responsibility? It so happens—but I never thought I would say something like this today!—that guilt would best name this beyond of responsibility. It is said all the time today that responsibility relieves one of all guilt. On the contrary, guilt is perhaps the beyond of all measurable responsibility. But let me stop with this. I can see Werner Hamacher shaking his head; he is no doubt thinking about Heidegger's *Schuldigkeit* as an attempt to think in terms that are too religious . . . Of course, we would need to discuss this notion of guilt a lot more. For the moment, to put it in a formal way, I would say that guilt presents itself in this way, as beyond responsibility.

I would like to add something regarding the performative. I agree completely with what you say about the performative, that it is annulled if the event is produced in conformity with a performing. But if the performative performs only sense, in the sense that I am trying to hear it, that is to say, the sense of a "to," the sense of an address, then at that moment—I am coming back to take something from the same tradition—I would say that the performative of the one who calls "Abraham" and of Abraham who responds "here I am"—and this is something you are quite familiar with—is a double performative that performs nothing other than the fact that they are responding to each other, after which their entire story begins . . . We could also consider another type of performative found in a certain mystical tradition, in Islam at least, namely, a performative whereby the faithful's profession of faith creates the content of faith. And thus, at the limit, it is in the profession of faith that God himself and his relationship to the world are created.

JD: This allows me to move toward the third question. The call to which one ultimately responds, beyond a determined, calculable, determinable demand, is what you refer to when you speak of sense. That is what sense is, the origin and the sense of sense. As for this indeterminate call, or at least this call that does not let itself be determined by a calculable object, by a calculable demand, I wonder if it is not a call to go, precisely, beyond sense. The call to give—give me love, give me this or that—this gift that is asked for, if it is to be a gift, must precisely have no sense, that is, it must not appear as such since as soon as it does it destroys itself. To use your word here: I wonder whether this call from as far as possible, this quasi-infinite call, does not in fact exceed sense instead of providing sense, as you suggest. This brings us back to the point you just raised: infinite responsibility as guilt or not. A tradition that we know well begins with original sin, but one finds traces of this all the way up to Heidegger and Levinas: before owing this or that, before incurring a debt or committing a fault, I must *respond*, this is the originary *Schuldigsein*; I am thus neither simply guilty nor responsible but at fault [*peccable*] or liable [*passible*]. Even before owing this or that or before having committed some fault or other, I am in some sense liable or at fault. I think you find this in Heidegger, and in Levinas in another way, when he speaks of an originary debt before any determined debt. The "here I am" is of this order. However powerful and respectable these thoughts may be, they perhaps belong, whether they recognize it or not, to a, say, biblical provenance. When I speak of infinite responsibility, it borders on this, it's very close to this, but I am at least trying—whether I am successful or not is another matter—to think a responsibility *for more than one* [à plus d'un], indeed, before more than one. There is more than one call, even when it comes, even if it came, from the same person; there is more than one, and I cannot respond infinitely, I cannot measure up to the infinite responsibility that is assigned to me by this "more than one call," coming from more than one or more than one place. There is here some incalculable, a sort of infinity, to come back to the problematic brought up yesterday. This infinity is not necessarily circumscribed by the tradition we just evoked. When I say "every other is every (bit) other" [*tout autre est tout autre*], this means that there is a multiplicity of others and thus a multiplicity of calls. I am equally responsible before each and every other, and this responsibility is not calculable. Of course, I am obliged to calculate (it's a *société à responsabilité limitée*, a limited liability partnership), I cannot respond as a finite singularity, I cannot respond to all the calls, but the call is infinite, and I am constantly trying to measure up to the immensity, to the incommensurability, to the infiniteness of this disseminated call, which is not the call of the one, of a one, of someone, but of more than one, more than one at once. Or else it is each time one, of course, irreplaceably so, but more than one unique, more than one irreplaceable—each time every (bit) other.

This remark leads me to the third series of questions I wanted to ask you. They bring us back to the so-called "deconstruction of Christianity." In short, who takes on today, who would take on or assume, the responsibility for a deconstruction of Christianity? To follow the thread of what you were saying earlier, it is obvious that if responsibility is unlimited that is because it is not simply the responsibility of a conscious, free, determined, subject but because it comes from further away or from higher up; it is older than I. But then also, the "one before whom" I must assume my responsibility is perhaps not yet formed. The one who addresses the call to you perhaps does not exist. This one is undetermined and is, perhaps, precisely to come. At that point, it is a question of a responsibility to be taken with regard to the "one who is coming and who has not yet come and who will perhaps not come." We come back to the problematic of messianicity, which we discussed this morning. I have some responsibility toward that which, those whom, I do not yet know. Not only the dead, who are no longer here, or who return in one form or another, as ghosts, but those who are not yet born. This enormous question could be illustrated by many concrete examples. In any case, one cannot abdicate a responsibility before those one does not know, before the one who is not yet born. Or who has been dead a long time without my even having known him.

With all the work you do on the notion of world, of creation, and so on, who takes responsibility for the "deconstruction of Christianity," and before whom? To make my questions more precise, since I want to ask them on the basis of your work and address them to you, I am going to read two passages that are particularly dense: I could read others, of course, if we had the time, but I chose these from *The Sense of the World,* where you say the following (I have chosen this passage because what is at issue is the question of sense, and of the "deconstruction of Christianity" with regard to sense):

> In truth, if one understands by *world* a "totality of signifyingness or significance [*significance*]," no doubt there is no philosophy that has thought a beyond of the world. The appearance of such a thought and of the contradiction it entails comes from the Christian sense of *world* as that which precisely lacks all sense or has its sense beyond itself. In this sense, moreover, sense itself [I am asking you to take responsibility for these claims—JD] is a specifically Christian determination or postulation that supposes a step beyond the *cosmos* to which *agathon* still belongs. To this very degree, that which we have to think henceforth under the title of sense can consist only in the abandonment of Christian sense or in an abandoned sense. Which one can also put like this: sense—if it is still or finally necessary to do justice to the obstinate request of this word [so, must one do justice? because you say "if," "if it is still necessary," and so the question is whether it is necessary—JD]—can proceed only from a deconstruction of Christianity.[5]

This last line calls for a footnote, and here is your note:

> Which signifies, to be precise, something other than a critique or a demolition: the bringing to light of that which will have been the agent of Christianity as the very form of the West, much more deeply than all religion and even as the self-deconstruction of religion, that is, the accomplishment of philosophy by Judeo-Platonism and Latinity, ontotheology as its own end, the "death of God" and the birth of the sense of the world as the abandonment without return and

without *Aufhebung* of all "christ" [you put "christ" in quotation marks—JD], that is, of all hypostasis of sense. It will of course be necessary to come back to this.[6]

The word *sense* seems to be, on the one hand, linked to this Christianity that must be abandoned. But once this Christianity has been abandoned, we nevertheless retain the word *sense*, dechristianized, as it were. It is still needed. It is and it is no longer the same word. In other words, you seem to want to save sense after its dechristianization, all the while saying, in other texts, that dechristianization is an operation of self-deconstruction, that is to say, still Christian: it saves itself in the sense it, in some way, loses. This is what I would like you to explain to us with regard to sense, with regard to the responsibility you yourself assume with regard to the word *sense* after Christianity, if one can say "after Christianity" or "beyond Christianity."

To this text, let me add another, and then I'll stop. It is in your most recent book, *The Creation of the World*: "Creation [obviously, as you well know, your use of the word *creation* is a provocation; if there is one word I will always hesitate to use, it is this one; it is precisely here that the question I asked earlier regarding the performative gets reposed or redeployed] forms, then, a nodal point in a 'deconstruction of monotheism,' insofar as such a deconstruction proceeds from monotheism itself [*monothéisme lui-même*]."[7] We've already talked about this word *même* ("itself, same"), and we can come back to it later. I take from Benveniste what seems to me an enlightening and highly significant observation, namely, that the word *même* itself [*lui-même*], wherever it appears, retains and reaffirms the memory of its etymological origin, that is, it refers, like *meisme* (*metipssimus*), to *ipse*, to the self [*soi*]. *Ipse* refers always to the self as to some authority, that of the master of the house, of the boss, of the head, the father or the husband, and so on. Benveniste cites many texts, and his point becomes clear: each time one uses the word *ipse*, one is implicitly designating a power, a masculine "I can," the sovereignty of the master of the house, of the husband, of the despot. There is the same implied meaning in every reference to ipseity and thus every reference to the word *même*, which implicitly contains it. Now, no philosophical discourse can do without the word *même*: we say *la chose même* ("the thing itself"), *ceci même* ("this itself, this very thing") when we are speaking about the essence that is *proper* to something, and each time we say *même* we are calling up, at least implicitly, the power, or more precisely, the authority of the master of the house, the masculine authority of the master and host. If there is thus something to deconstruct, this is it, this word *même*, this word it-self [*lui-"même"*],which is in philosophical language everywhere at home [*chez lui*].

You continue:

> such a deconstruction proceeds from monotheism itself, and perhaps is its most active resource. The unique god [now, if anyone is himself (*lui-même*), it's indeed that, the unique god—JD], whose unicity is the correlate of the creating act, cannot precede its creation any more than it can subsist above it or apart from it in some way. It merges with it: merging with it, it withdraws in it, and withdrawing there it empties itself there, emptying itself it is nothing other than the opening of this void.[8]

I would like to know if, in fact, the void, the kenosis, is still there or not. You continue: "Only the opening is divine, but the divine is nothing more than the opening. The opening is neither the foundation nor the origin. Nor is the opening a sort of receptacle or prior expanse for the things of the world."[9] Are you not, in some way, replacing the fullness of the unique god of monotheism by the opening to which this god must himself yield? And so we find your ever-present concern for the opening—even your definition of freedom as something that is not the predicate of a subject but the opening of the free, as Heidegger says, the fact of appearing, which is what leads you sometimes to say that a tree is free, simply insofar as it is in the open and in appearing. In this opening, everything shifts: we go from the sense of monotheism, of Christianity, to a sense of an after Christianity or a sense that exceeds the sense of Christianity. Let me stop at this point and reformulate my question, which is certainly not an objection to you and is not a question that I do not ask myself or that does not worry me. I should have said this earlier, in the discussion with Roberto Esposito, concerning the question of the messianic: as concerns the opening, that is to say, the appearing of what unveils or reveals itself as truth, might it not be linked, by speaking a bit of German, to the distinction Heidegger makes between *Offenbarung*—the place of biblical, historical revelation—and *Offenbarkeit*, that is, the possibility of *opening* [apérité], the possi*bility* of this *Offenbarung*, a possi*bility* that Heidegger of course says is more originary? One would first have to think, to have already thought, revealability (*Offenbarkeit*) in order then to determine revelation. This couple *Offenbarkeit/Offenbarung*, just like the couple messianicity/messianism, in fact, is a diabolical couple, very difficult to master. One cannot decide whether the condition of *Offenbarung* was *Offenbarkeit*, that is, the opening of the revealable in which a historical revelation was inscribed, or whether, on the contrary, it was an *Offenbarung*, that is, an event that has taken place, unforeseeably, that opened revealability to itself, that opened the opening. In other words, according to the latter logic, it is because there was the event of historical revelation, historical revelations, and religions that *it* [ça] opened up, that one could think the opening of the open rather than the contrary.

I do not have a decidable or decided answer to this question. I have the feeling of being caught or of oscillating in that between. My uneasiness is here an uneasiness of responsibility: Is responsibility to be found in *Offenbarkeit* or in *Offenbarung*? Theologians or traditional believers will say that, if you think *Offenbarkeit*, it is because there was *Offenbarung*, and our responsibility is to take into account, to take on the inheritance, of this *Offenbarung* in order to think *Offenbarkeit*, which is contrary to what Heidegger does. In the Heideggerian style, one says, on the contrary, that the true responsibility of thinking, that what is to be thought, is *Offenbarkeit*, that the *Offenbarung* is not of the order of thought or of philosophy. Hence Heidegger says that Christianity has nothing to do with philosophy, that it is madness for thinking; you know those texts . . . Well, there again, it's a question of responsibility with regard to sense. Let me stop here.

J-LN: Okay, let's begin from the end.

First, the question is that of revelation. Without returning to the terrible circle you describe, which is undeniable, that of *Offenbarung/Offenbarkeit*, one must recall nonetheless that this circle has been marked in philosophy since Hegel. Hegel says this in *Lectures on the Proofs of the Existence of God*: "What is revealed [he is talking, of course, about the religion that he calls "revealed"] is simply this, that God is the revealable." And it is not by chance that, at a certain moment, this came to be lodged in philosophy, which opens for me onto the exigency to think in terms of the deconstruction of monotheism, which is to say, in terms of the indissoluble relation between philosophy and revealed religion within our origin. We must reappropriate this history, precisely because the triple monotheism is marked through and through by this couple *Offenbarung* and *Offenbarkeit*, and because philosophy seems to have defined itself against this but can probably not rid itself of it. In other words, what is revealed is that there is a revealability that is completely inaugural, archi-originary, of what is called God, but this is in fact revealed only through a revelation, a revelation that does not take one form but two, and then three . . .

JD: And it's not over. . . .

J-LN: It's not over . . . That, I don't know . . . Maybe, but maybe no longer in the form of the same kind of event, that is, a founding event of religion . . . Because even in this aspect of a founding event—one cannot not notice this—monotheism has repeated itself. I really think there is no comparable example of this. There is no other religion that has felt the need to re-reveal itself each time anew, becoming another religion and yet refounding the same one. There is perhaps only one thing that resembles this, very curiously, and that is philosophy in its history. Because, in the end, each philosopher behaves like Mohammed vis-à-vis Christ or Moses, or like Christ vis-à-vis Moses. And at the same time, philosophers as a whole also behave in this way vis-à-vis religion, which obviously complicates the entire issue, since philosophy also says that it reveals the true revealability of what offers itself as revelation. That's a first point.

A second point, going back a bit further in your remarks, concerns the opening. The opening, I grant you, is a rather problematic word, not unlike another word I used a long time ago and that continues to follow me wherever I go, the word *partage* (sharing [out]). The opening, with its connotations of generosity as well as of apparition and revelation, must always be brought back, it seems to me, if one still wants to use this word, to that which is the condition of an opening, namely, the contour. The opening is not just some infinite gaping: in fact, there is no infinite opening. It might be possible to say, we perhaps in fact must say, that the opening is always opening *to* infinity but it itself is not infinite—and from that point of view I am really not very comfortable with the theme of the Open in Heidegger, with a certain Heideggerian Hölderlinism of the Open, in the Open, which is moreover the Free . . . No, the opening is what calls for its contour in order to open up, just as the mouth opens and gives its contour and thus itself takes on contours; one would have to think about the mouth when it sings, which would in fact bring us back to resonance. In other words, what else is the demand, the call, or the injunction for an opening if not the demand or injunction to have to trace contours, and thus forms, for a revelation, contours, it might simply be said, for something of the Open in general to present itself? Otherwise, nothing would present itself at all. This seems in certain respects to have escaped Heidegger, in spite of what he says about art, especially in his little text "Art and Space": the necessity of the contour . . .

JD: Heidegger insists a great deal on the contour, on the *horos*, the limit . . .

J-LN: Yes, but with him it always seems to be a closing off rather than that which, precisely, opens up.

But let's come back to the question of Christianity. The heart of the issue is that you want to make me contradict myself because I would be saving sense from Christianity, a sense that would itself be entirely and essentially Christian. Well, then, yes, of course, I would gladly admit that the whole problem is to be located right there. That is, our origin [*provenance*] is indeed made up of this monotheism, on the one hand, but, on the other hand—and it is important for me to stress this, since we tend to consider it far too little—this triple monotheism is not itself independent of philosophy. And the question of *sense*, whether we want to retain this word or not, cannot but concern philosophy and, through it, Christianity and/or monotheism.

Behind all of this, in fact, behind what makes possible or even necessary an interest in what I have called the "deconstruction of Christianity," an expression whose terms already create an alliance between philosophical and religious markers, I think there is, at the very least, a contemporaneity and, at most, perhaps, a co-historiality (to speak like Heidegger) of philosophy and monotheism, with all the enormous differences that would have to be analyzed.

That means that everything can be brought back, by tracing back this history in our at once religious and philosophical origin, to what we were discussing earlier, that is, to the gift of an abandonment. After all, what I pointed to earlier in the figure of original sin is also, let's not forget, what makes Greek tragedy possible. For the gods give to Greek man measure, *horos*, and so on, but also *hybris*. And tragedy is also the gods' doing. Thus all of this constitutes our origin as a world that can be called non-religious insofar as it is non-polytheist, non-sacrificial . . . that is to say, as a world in which revelation is not simply what comes in addition but what constitutes the very thing that, through philosophico-theological revelation, gives in general the form of presence when it is no longer simply given as presence.

In polytheism presence is given, at least to a certain point, in a sort of assurance: there are gods, and in such a world I would say that there is only negotiation. One negotiates with the gods, if we may be allowed such a crude and all too rapid synopsis, one that should then leave some room for a return to what is perhaps the link or the hyphen between something of the sacred before and something after the event of the Western advent.

In these conditions, sense, as I try to say in the text you brought up—or as I tried to say, since it's a rather old text, which I do not use as an excuse, though it's true that things have evolved quite a bit since then—sense, which seems to me to be the very element of this entire tradition, designates for me nothing other than the lifting up [*levée*] of this sending [*envoi*], of this call, coming from and signaling toward presence as absented—to put it this way for now. That is what is at stake in the withdrawal of the gods: the sense of an absenting. And the triple monotheism plays a role here that is obviously completely double: a role, on the one hand, of reinstalling presence, assurance, and so on, and on the other hand, on the contrary, of deepening the absenting, as we can see in all the mystical traditions of the three religions.

If I say "mystical traditions," it must be recalled that this notion of absencing also runs through some of the less mystical thoughts and workings of these monotheisms, some of their most banal aspects, in which, in certain respects, the sense of absencing is linked, in spite of everything, to what we normally designate by the name *religion*, or *religious institution*.

This sense is at the same time, let me repeat it, joined, very intimately joined—Christianity first bears witness to this conjunction, and then Islam too, though in a different way, as well as Judaism, at least after the advent of Christianity—to what we call philosophy. And so all of this is always a question about the same thing, "how did the West reveal itself to itself?" or "how is it always the revelation to itself of what its name means, the West, the Occident, the setting sun? How is it the revelation to itself of obscurity?"

You are going to say: to itself [*à lui-même*]—that's what brings us back to the same [*même*]. Except that I would say: Isn't it the god of monotheism who, whatever form it may take, when it truly is what it is, if it "is," destroys its own "sameness" [*mêmeté*]? Which is not even [*même*] the same as itself [*le même que lui-même*]? After all, when I speak of this, I always have in mind Eckhart's line, and if I had a motto, if I had to give myself one, it would no doubt be this line of Eckhart's: "Let us pray to God that we may be free of God." I realize that this line is a real trap, since it's a question of praying to God—unless we say "let us pray (without naming God) that we may be free," but then we need to know what praying without praying to God means. I could cite other phrases from certain Jewish or Muslim mystics . . .

FG: And yet you've written: "If we must someday go beyond our atheism, it will be in order no longer even to pray to God to deliver us from God."

J-LN: Yes, you just nailed it! That's just the kind of answer Jacques was looking for! But there remains a question, or a void. To explain what I mean, I could quote Blanchot, whose name I wanted to evoke earlier in order to honor him, especially since just yesterday Monique Antelme conveyed to me his greetings. I am sorry I don't have *The Infinite Conversation* here. You'll find there a very beautiful note in which Blanchot designates a task that he does not call "deconstruction of Christianity" but that he says must not be satisfied with any, let us say, secularization or demythologization, indeed, any atheization. I think he mentions Feuerbach in this context, but, he says, refusing Feuerbach's move to replace God by man, it is a matter of "something completely other," a matter of doing or placing something completely other . . . "*in that very spot.*" In the end, I may be trying to say nothing other than this, namely, that there is a certain spot, a certain place and a certain time as the place and time of . . . let's say, the divine, revelation, the open, if we can put it like that, or sense.

JD: We don't have much time left. Just one final question. We can leave it in its virtuality. It would concern decision, the concept of decision, for example, in *The Experience of Freedom*, where you say of decisions: "decision appears: each time, we decide on a writing, we decide on a writing of writing, and therefore we decide on writing and on the sense in its offering and withdrawal. Sharing voices: never one single voice, the voice of sense *is* the decision, each time, of a singular voice. Freedom."[10]

Each time we speak of responsibility in the tradition, what is implied is decision and freedom, the freedom to decide. The response, the sense of response or of "responding" that is found in responsibility always implies decision and freedom, freedom in general, including the one you talk about, with all the transformations you make this word undergo, which I do not have the time to recall here.

My question is thus the following: What would you think of the claim, a claim I am often tempted by, according to which decision, if there is any, a decision that makes something happen, that would not in fact be the expression of my performative power, a decision that would not simply be the deployment of my possibilities, that would measure up to my impossibility, a decision, then, that is always not mine but the other's, is a passive decision, "my" decision is passive—the decision is passive, it is the other's, and I must assume responsibility for a decision I do not make, that is not mine, that is the other's, and in relation to which I am passive, as if with regard to an event? This is madness, isn't it? But I believe it to be as ineluctable as thought, as the beyond of that old couple active/passive.

Having advanced this proposition, I would have liked, though we don't have time, to come back to a major axis or axiomatic of Western thought, or at least of post-Cartesian thought, as far as responsibility is concerned. It stipulates—and this is the question of man that I am asking you—that man is naturally capable of decision, of responsibility, insofar as he is capable of *responding*, whereas the animal, the non-human living being, what we so crudely designate with the word *animal*, does not respond. This is a Cartesian tradition that runs all the way up to Heidegger, Lacan, and Levinas; I don't have the time to show this here (I do so elsewhere). The "animal," it is said, does not respond, it only *reacts*. It *reacts* precisely to a program; it reacts to stimuli. It has, of course, a sort of language; it communicates, it has signs, but these signs are reactions and never constitute responses. I find this distinction to be more than dubious and tenuous; it is, and we could show this in a thousand ways, though I don't have the time to do this, *false* for many animals. Moreover, and this is the point I wanted to underscore in the logic of what I've said up until now, nothing will ever be able to guarantee us, by means of a theoretical knowledge and a determinate judgment certain of themselves, that my response, that the response given, that the responsibility that is assumed, is of the order of responsibility and not reaction; that is, nothing will ever be able to guarantee us that some reaction is not entering into the so-called human response. We are dealing here, of course, with the distinction [*partage*], within the living, between what is stupidly [*bêtement*] called the animal in general and the proper of man. In other words, isn't asking the question of responsibility, as everyone does, with such obstinacy and by referring, at least implicitly, to the ethics of response, to freedom and decision in the traditional sense, already to circumscribe this question in a metaphysical anthropology that is more and more naïve from the standpoint of positive knowledge? We've known this for a long time now, but it's becoming more and more glaring to anyone who spends just a bit of time thinking about the organization of certain so-called animal species. In other words, to what extent can we trust this distinction between response and reaction, whose most straightforward articulations are to be found in Descartes, though also in Lacan? (We cannot show this here, but I think we could.) That is my question: What do you think here of my belief? Of what I assume, of what I presume? Namely, that all belief, all assurance with regard to this distinction between *responding* and *reacting*, in other words, all awareness I claim to have that I am responding in one place and reacting in another, and that one can rigorously determine the difference between a response and a reaction, is not only philosophically deconstructible, criticizable, dubious, for thought and for knowledge, but the first *ethical abdication*? From the moment when I believe I know (and when I trust this presumed knowledge) where responsibility is and where reaction is, I am already in a system of *assurance à responsabilité limitée*; I know what responsibility is, thus I know what has to be done; I know what I must do and what I can do as a human being. This so-called knowledge, which thereby subjects my undertakings and my actions to some knowledge, programs them and, as a result, instead of being the condition of an ethics worthy of the name, constitutes the first abdication, the first and most presumptuous forswearing [*parjure*]. This blind confidence in the distinction between the human and the animal, like the confidence given more generally to the distinction between responding and reacting, is not only a philosophical and scientific abdication but an ethical one. And that is the whole question of the animal, which you know has preoccupied me a great deal elsewhere, and about which I am only able to say a word here.

This morning, after Jean-Clet Martin's presentation, it was a question of extending the concept of *Dasein* to technical objects, to things, and so on. It is obvious that in this great tradition only a *Dasein*, in the Heideg-gerian sense, can be said to be responsible. There is no responsibility that can be attributed to animals, for example. Nor before what are called animals.

J-LN: Of course, since I would say that to be responsible and to have a world, in Heidegger's terms, are the same thing. They coincide. And since, for Heidegger, the animal is poor in world, as we know, and the stone has no world, then, of course . . . In Jean-Clet Martin's presenta-tion, there was the lizard that comes from Heidegger . . .

JD: According to this logic, by accrediting the distinction between reaction and response, we end up with statements such as Lacan's, for example, where responsibility and ethics, like criminality, presuppose the law as the "proper of man." Cruelty itself is human, only human, even so-called bestial cruelty. Only man can be cruel, and always toward his fellow human being, because he is under the law. As a result, every other living being is considered foreign to the law and so cannot even be cruel. But we can then commit the worst acts of violence upon other living beings without being ascribed any crime or cruelty, without having any responsibility with regard to these other living beings. These are the con-sequences that can be drawn from this logic.

J-LN: Let's note, in this regard, that our ethico-juridical world is in the process of changing with respect to cruelty toward animals.

JD: There would be a lot to say here. Are there animals in your world? There are, of course, but do you give them an essential place?

J-LN: No, not at all. In fact, I was going to start there . . . I agree with you entirely that I do not reserve any special place for animals, but I do for living beings, and there is, let me remind you, somewhere in one of my texts the tree that is free . . .

JD: If there are living beings, okay, if there are animals . . .

J-LN: Of course. I grant you that one poor tree, whose species is not even identified, is not much to pull in the entire world of living beings. I was even going to say to you, to begin with, that when you talk about the animal, I often say to myself two things. First of all, I am a bit skeptical, and I say to myself: "What's come over him here, what is this . . . isn't this just a bit much?" And then I often say to myself: "There are more urgent things than this." But then, on the other hand, I say to myself . . .

JD: My interest in animals extends also to human animals. You see what I mean . . .

J-LN: Then I already feel better. I was afraid you were going to institute a law that allowed you to be cruel to me but not to your cat.

JD: That's the suspicion or accusation that people like Luc Ferry make against all those who take an interest in animals for animals' sake: in the end, they prefer animals to man, and the Nazis did as well, and so on. That's the typical argument that comes out of this kind of humanism. I have responded to it elsewhere.

J-LN: In this regard, I myself am completely empirical: "We cannot do everything, and so Jacques is taking care of the animals, well and good, to each his own herd, and the cows will be well cared for!" So then leave men for me . . .

JD: Be my guest . . .

J-LN: No, but seriously, I say these stupid and completely off-topic things because I need some way to approach what's at stake.

But let me note that what comes immediately to mind is a whole series of observations concerning the fact that what you are saying—which, of course, I agree with entirely, this whole questioning of the distinction between response and reaction—today plays a considerable role in the decisions of justice, this whole zone of indecision, which is of course always settled by decisions. But such decisions are made by relying upon the couple reaction-response, by saying, for example, "He is not responsible because all he did was react," and, in the last analysis, that is what a certain attribution of illness means. I grant you this entirely, but I say to myself that I can understand this only by trying to go back before [*en-deçà*]—I say go back before; that's probably not the only figure to use here, but let's move on—the couple reaction-response, and thus before the separation man-animal, and then we are headed, through an anam-nestic route, straight back to Egypt, for example. And then, behind Egypt, we will get back to totemism . . . and we are at that moment . . .

JD: We have never left totemism . . .

J-LN: Okay, but that then means that, between man and the animal, what you are asking for must be fundamentally less a sort of equaling or balancing of the scales than, first of all, a thinking of what refers each of these two to the other. This then brings me back to what I earlier called resonance. Perhaps, behind—or ahead of—the distinction between response and reaction there is resonance. And when you say that we are still in totemism, I would at least say that our civilization itself has never completely left behind the resonance between man and the animal. There are plenty of dogs, ever since Ulysses' dog, and cats, including those of Baudelaire, to attest to this. I thus have nothing to argue against this, nothing to object to you on this subject, except to point out that you are dealing at this point with something that has to do with . . .

FG: I think we are going to have to leave the room . . .

JD: Right away?

FG: We've been asked to free up the room . . .

JD: I thought there was going to be some discussion with the audience . . .

J-LN: I thought the same thing . . .

FG: Let me say a word about this. As moderator of this session, I am going to have to make a decision that is at once passive, authoritarian, and frustrating . . . At the same time, it seems to me, what we were expecting will not have taken place exactly as we had expected and what we did not expect will perhaps have taken place, in a different way, through what we have heard and what has been addressed to us . . . It seems to me, in any case, that there will be many of us who, in spite of or through these frustrations, will be very grateful for what took place, for what will have been given to us or abandoned for us, and who will take the time—an infinite time—to let this resonate in us and among us. Thank you.

Notes

TRANSLATORS' PREFACE

1. This lecture, the last that Derrida would give in France, was published under the title "Le souverain bien—ou l'Europe en mal de souveraineté: La conférence de Strasbourg du 8 juin 2004" in the journal *Cités*, special issue *Derrida politique—La déconstruction de la souveraineté (puissance et droit)*, no. 30 (2007): 103–40. The lecture is based almost entirely, with the exception of a long introduction, on the first session (of December 12, 2001) of Derrida's seminar *The Beast and Sovereign*, vol. 1, trans. Geoffrey Bennington (Chicago: University of Chicago Press, 2009), 1–31 . The lecture was also published, without the long introduction of the Strasbourg conference, in the proceedings of the 2002 Cerisy conference, *La démocratie à venir*, ed. Marie-Louise Mallet (Paris: Galilée, 2004), 433–56. It was also presented, with a different introduction, at a conference in Coimbra, Portugal, in 2003 (La souveraineté: Critique, déconstruction, apories: Autour de la pensée de Jacques Derrida) and published, first separately in a bilingual edition, under the title *Le souverain Bien/O soberano Bem*, trans. Fernanda Bernardo (Viseu: Palimage Editores, 2004), and then in the proceedings of the conference *Jacques Derrida à Coimbra/Derrida em Coimbra*, ed. Fernando Bernardo (Viseu: Palimage Editores, 2005), 75–105.

2. *"Le lieu dit: Strasbourg,"* in *Penser à Strasbourg* (Galilée and Ville de Strasbourg, 2004), 31–59.

3. [Derrida playfully refers to himself, Jean-Luc Nancy, and Philippe Lacoue-Labarthe as "the Three Musketeers" who founded the collection La philosophie en effet with Éditions Galilée. Following a suggestion by his friend Elisabeth Roudinesco, Derrida was reading the adventure novel by Alexandre Dumas during the last year of his life. In chapter 3, we see Derrida again making reference to the Dumas novel, suggesting that he, François Châtelet, Jean-Pierre Faye, and Dominique Lecourt were the *four* musketeers who founded the International College of Philosophy.—Trans.]

4. The four students were Perrine Marthelot, Nicolas Heitz, Benjamin Mamie, and Stanislas Jullien.

5. "Dialogue entre Jacques Derrida, Philippe Lacoue-Labarthe et Jean-Luc Nancy," in *Rue Descartes*, no. 52 (Paris: Presses Universitaires de France, 2006), 86–99.

6. "Ouverture," discussion with Jean-Luc Nancy, in *Rue Descartes*, no. 45, *Les 20 ans du Collège international de philosophie* (2004): 26–55.

7. "Responsabilité—du sens à venir," conversation with Jean-Luc Nancy, in *Sens en tous sens: Autour des travaux de Jean-Luc Nancy* (Paris: Galilée, 2004), 165–200.

1. THE PLACE NAME(S)—STRASBOURG (2004)

1. [Derrida is obviously responding here to the title of the conference, "Penser à Strasbourg," which means at once thinking *of* and thinking *in* Strasbourg. The French title of Derrida's essay, "Le lieu dit: Strasbourg," can be heard in several different ways. First, a *lieu-dit* is a place-name, a term used to designate a locality or small geographical area. When *dit* is taken as the past participle of *dire*, the phrase can mean "The place called or named Strasbourg," and when *dit* is taken as the third person singular form of the present tense, with Strasbourg as its object, it means "the place speaks, names, or dictates Strasbourg." The title can thus be heard as a translation of the epigraph that follows, "Der Ort sagt," which comes from Hölderlin's translation of Creon's words in Sophocles' *Antigone*. Derrida quotes these words, along with Philippe Lacoue-Labarthe's translation of them—"C'est le lieu qui me dicte"—at the beginning of "*Ex abrupto*," trans. Peggy Kamuf, in *Psyche: Inventions of the Other*, vol. 1, ed. Peggy Kamuf and Elizabeth Rottenberg (Stanford, Calif.: Stanford University Press, 2007), 262–63. Kamuf translates the phrase as "It is the place that dictates to me."—Trans.]

2. *Penser l'Europe à ses frontières* (Paris: Éditions de l'Aube, 1993).

3. [A TGV (*train à grande vitesse*) or high speed train was finally established between Paris and Strasbourg in 2007.—Trans.]

4. Jacques Derrida, *The Post Card: From Socrates to Freud and Beyond*, trans. Alan Bass (Chicago: University of Chicago Press, 1987), 189.

5. [GREPH (Groupe de recherche sur l'enseignement philosophique), founded by Derrida and others in 1975, tried to protect the teaching of philosophy in the final year of high school and even extend its teaching to earlier grades. Derrida speaks at some length about GREPH in Chapter 3. See also the many references to GREPH in *Who's Afraid of Philosophy? Right to Philosophy 1*, trans. Jan Plug (Stanford, Calif.: Stanford University Press, 2002), and *Eyes of the University, Right to Philosophy 2*, trans. Jan Plug and others (Stanford, Calif.: Stanford University Press, 2004). See the translator's foreword to *Eyes of the University* for a succinct account of the origins of both GREPH and the International College of Philosophy.—Trans.]

2. DISCUSSION BETWEEN JACQUES DERRIDA, PHILIPPE LACOUE-LABARTHE, AND JEAN-LUC NANCY (2004)

1. [See section 74 of *Being and Time*.—Trans.]

2. [Derrida writes in *Of Grammatology*, trans. Gayatri Chakravorty Spivak (Baltimore: The Johns Hopkins University Press, 1976), 69, "all graphemes are of a testamentary essence."—Trans.]

3. [Jean-Luc Nancy is referring here to the comments Derrida made after each of the student presentations during the day of doctoral studies organized by the Department of Philosophy at the Marc Bloch University.—Trans.]

4. On the question of the animal, see Jacques Derrida's *The Animal That Therefore I Am*, trans. David Wills (New York: Fordham University Press, 2008), as well as the two volumes of Derrida's final seminars, *The Beast and the Sovereign*, vols. 1 and 2, trans. Geoffrey Bennington (Chicago: University of Chicago Press, 2009, 2011).

3. OPENING (2003)

1. [In French a *passeur* is someone who ferries passengers across a river or brings them across borders.—Trans.]

2. [This is the report written in 1982 by François Châtelet, Jacques Derrida, Jean-Pierre Faye, and Dominique Lecourt in anticipation of the founding of the College. It has been published as *Le rapport bleu: Les sources historiques et théoriques du Collège international de philosophie* (Presses Universitaires de France, 1998).—Trans.]

3. I am here reconstituting very poorly, from memory and very schematically, the argument I had developed during the anniversary session of the College.—J-LN.

4. [High school teachers are released from a certain percentage of their normal teaching load when teaching a course at the College.—Trans.]

5. [Jan Plug writes in his Introduction to *Eyes of the University*, x: "With the announcement of the Réforme Haby—named after then minister of national education, René Haby—which set out to curtail the teaching of philosophy in French secondary schools, the group's work took on new urgency. GREPH fought not only to maintain philosophy in the lycée but to extend it, to have it begin before the final year, or Terminale, in which it had traditionally been taught." Plug goes on to offer a clear account of the work of GREPH during the last 1970s, of the Estates General held on June 16 and 17, 1979, and then of the founding of the International College of Philosophy on October 10, 1983—Trans.]

6. [Jean-Pierre Chevènement was François Mitterrand's minister of research and industry from 1981 to 1983 and then minister of national education from 1984 to 1986.—Trans.]

7. [Established in 1530, the Collège de France is a non–degree-granting institution of higher learning and research. It offers lectures that are free and open to the

public on a variety of topics in both the sciences and the humanities. Originally created in 1941 and then refounded under its current name in 1975, the École des Hautes Études en Sciences Sociales (School for Advanced Studies in the Social Sciences) is an institution for research and higher learning that offers master's and doctoral degrees through its forty-seven research centers and thirteen doctoral programs.—Trans.]

4. RESPONSIBILITY—OF THE SENSE TO COME (2002)

1. [The title given to this discussion, "Responsabilité—du sens à venir," can be heard in several different ways. It can be read as a title and subtitle—"Responsibility: Of the Sense to Come"—or as a single title meaning "Responsibility of" or "Responsibility for" "the sense to come." There is also the intimation of "Responsibility—in the sense to come," that is, responsibility in a sense that has not yet arrived or been understood.—Trans.]

2. [Nancy is referring to the children's game "pass the slipper" (*le furet*).—Trans.]

3. [Other speakers at this two-day conference organized by Francis Guibal and Jean-Clet Martin around the work of Jean-Luc Nancy included Alexander García-Düttmann, Roberto Esposito, Werner Hamacher, and Catherine Malabou.—Trans.]

4. [*Khâgne* is the second year of preparatory classes in humanities for entrance to the École Normale Supérieure.—Trans.]

5. Jean-Luc Nancy, *The Sense of the World*, trans. Jeffrey S. Libbrett (Minneapolis: University of Minnesota Press, 1997), 54–55.

6. Ibid., 183n50.

7. Jean-Luc Nancy, *The Creation of the World; or, Globalization*, trans. François Raffoul and David Pettigrew (Albany: State University of New York Press, 2007), 70.

8. Ibid.

9. Ibid.. trans. modified.

10. Jean-Luc Nancy, *The Experience of Freedom*, trans. Bridget McDonald (Stanford, Calif.: Stanford University Press, 1993), 152.